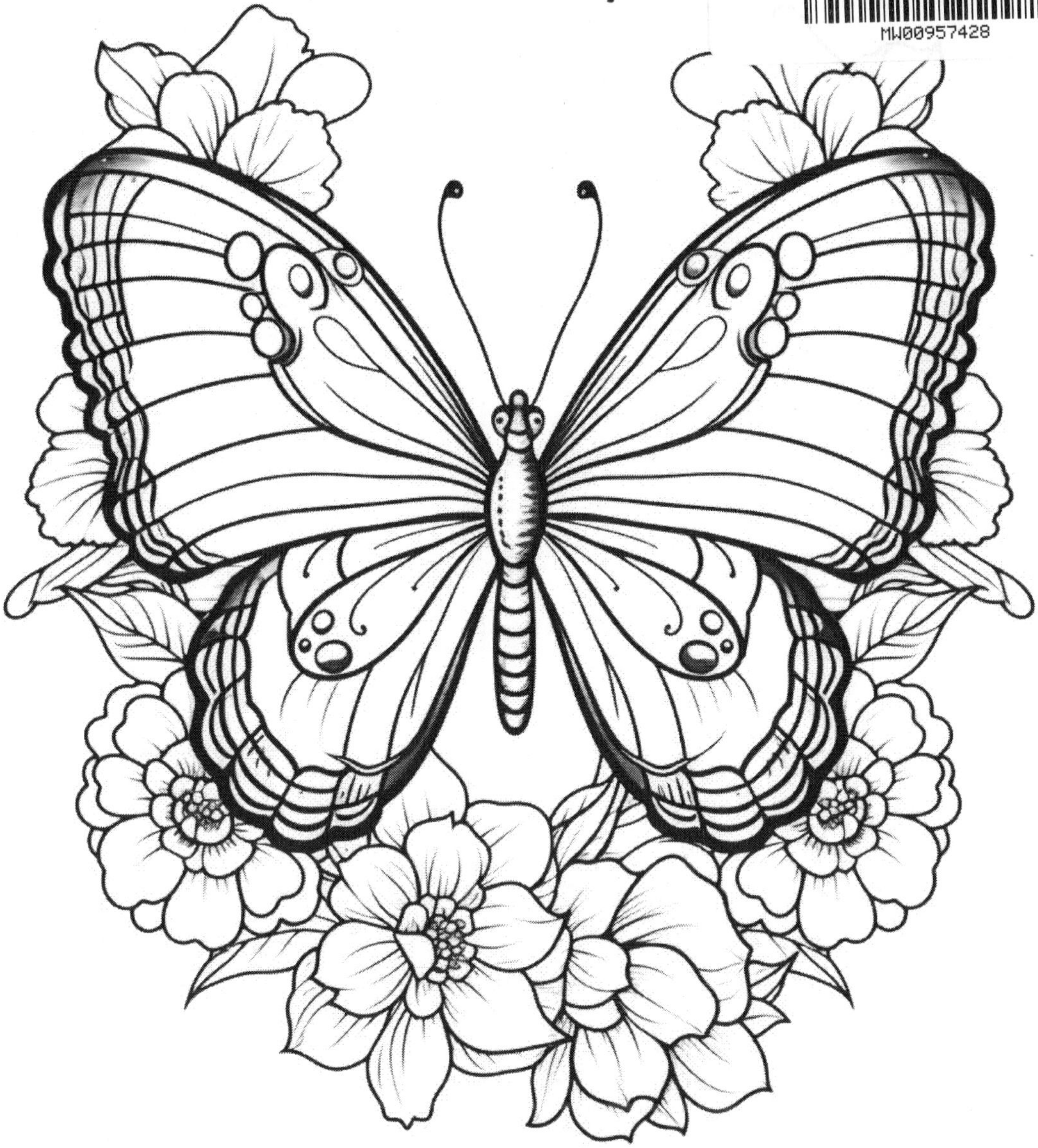

This Book Belongs To:

# COLOR TEST

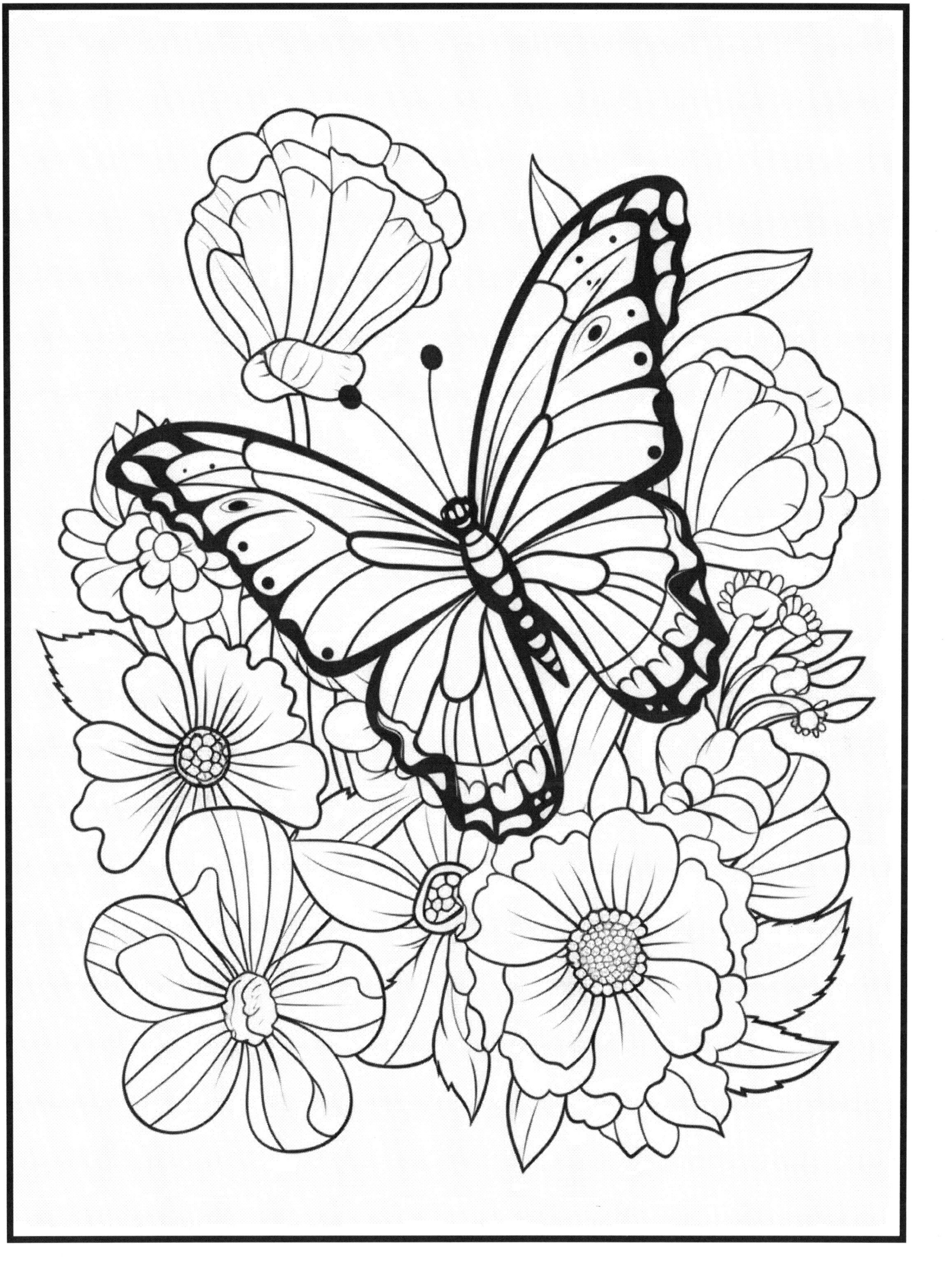

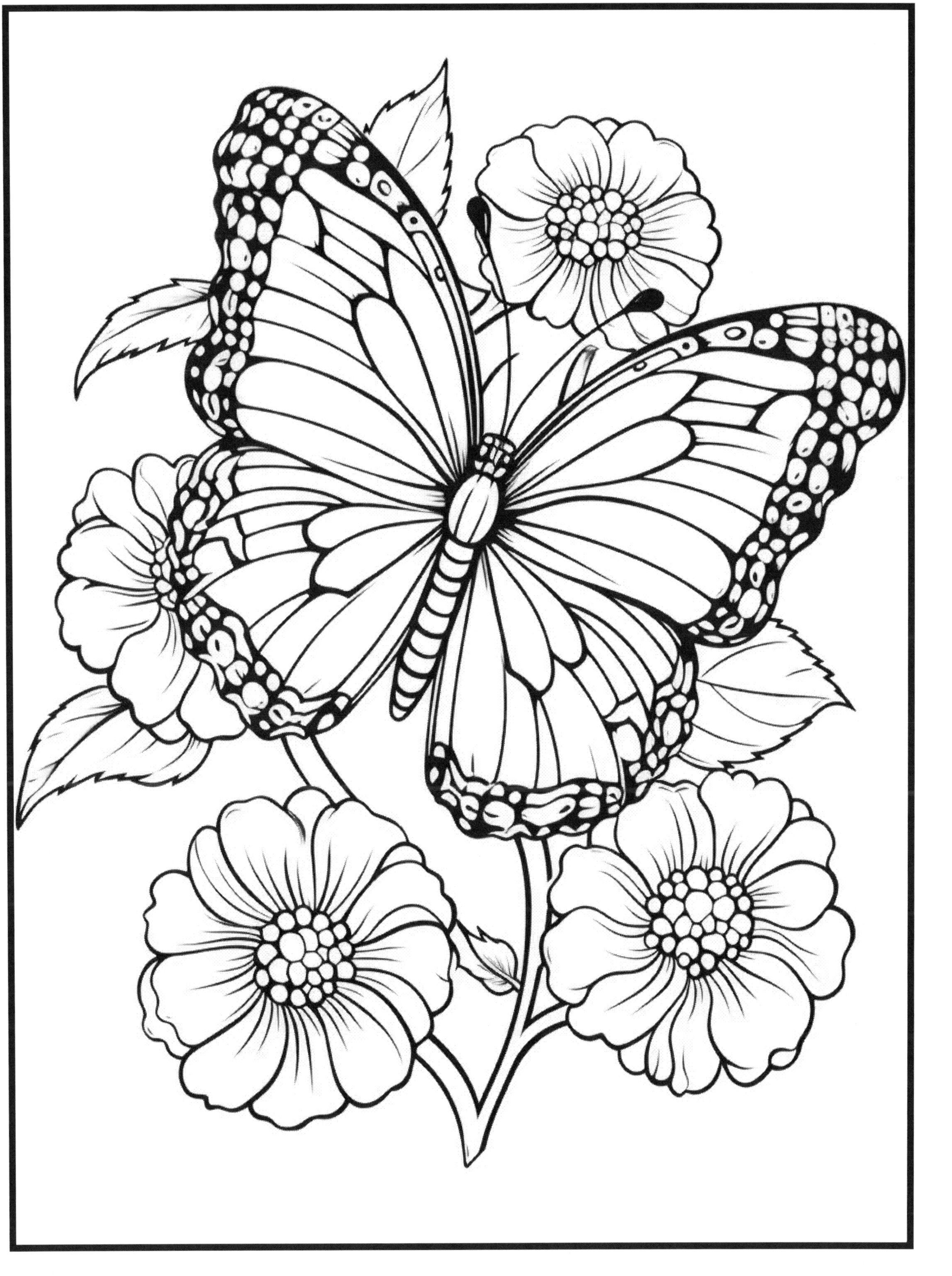

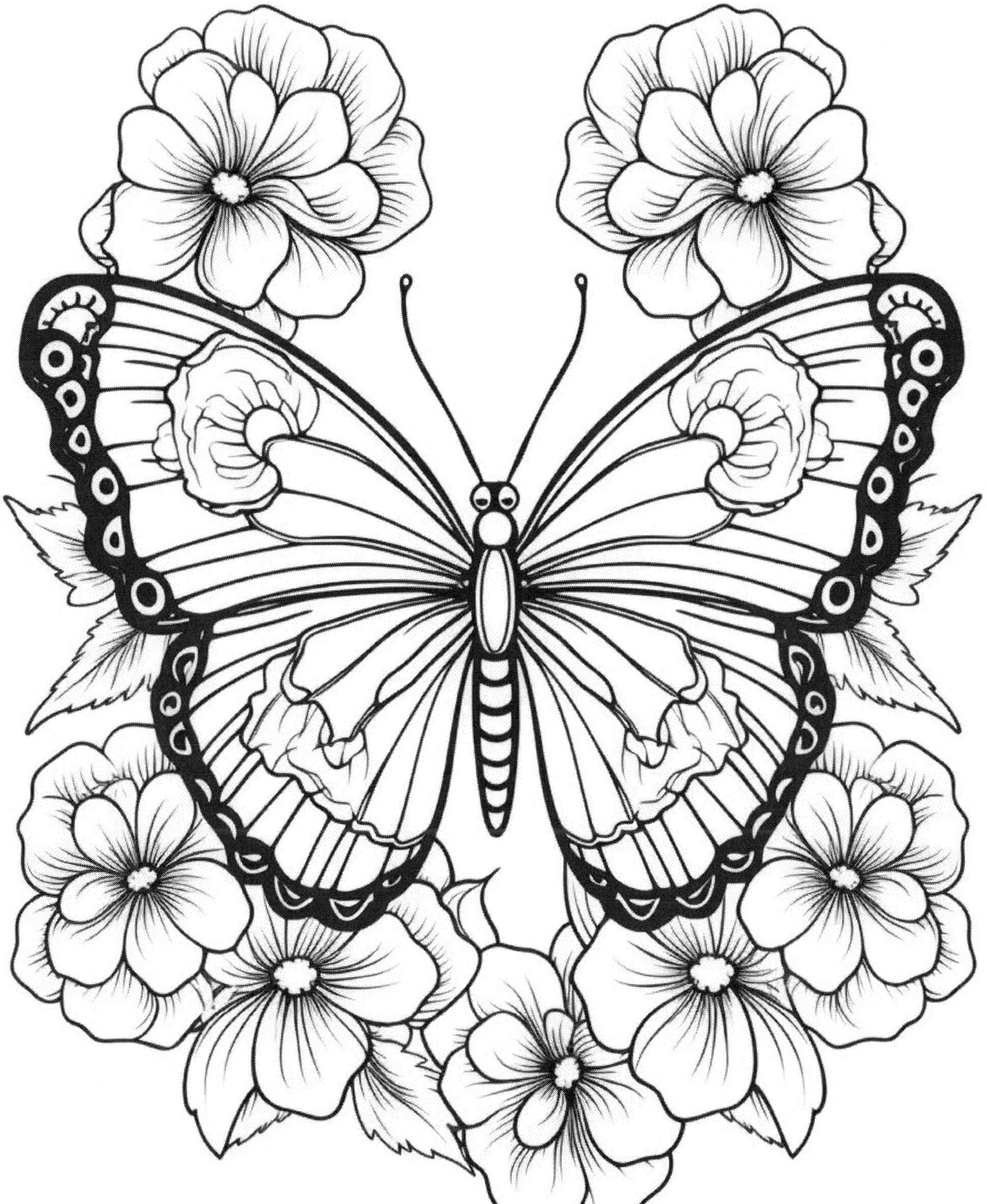

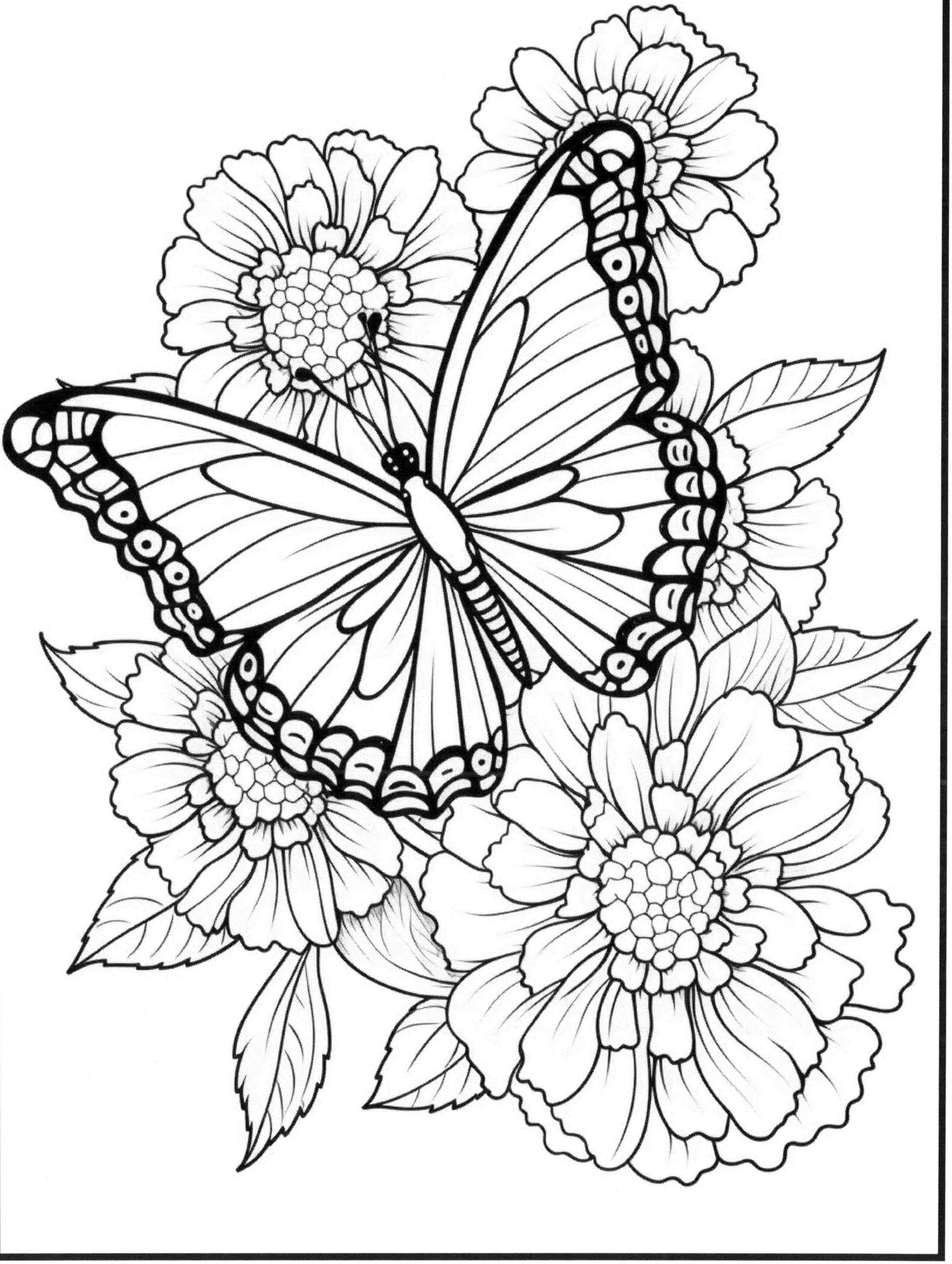

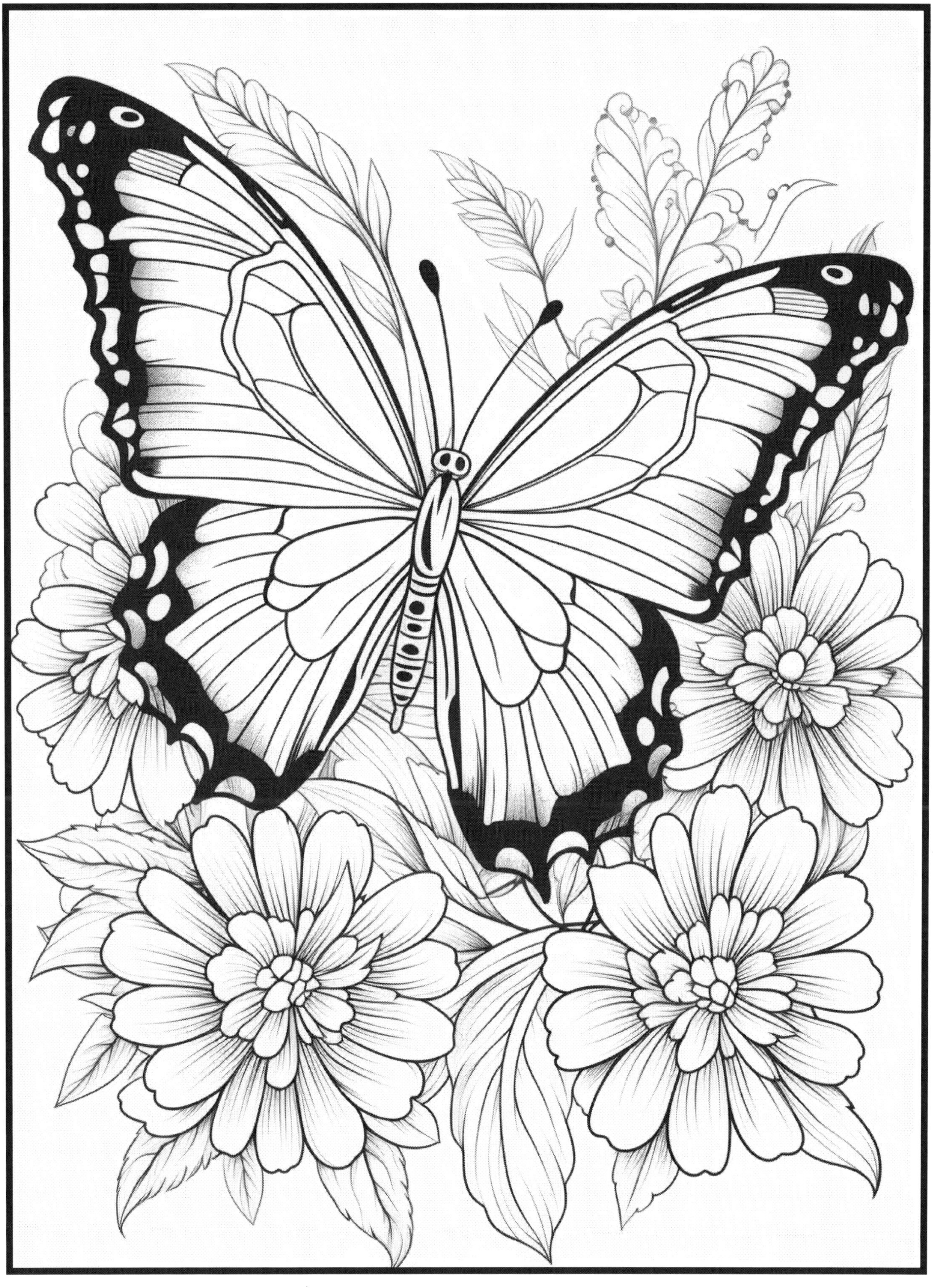

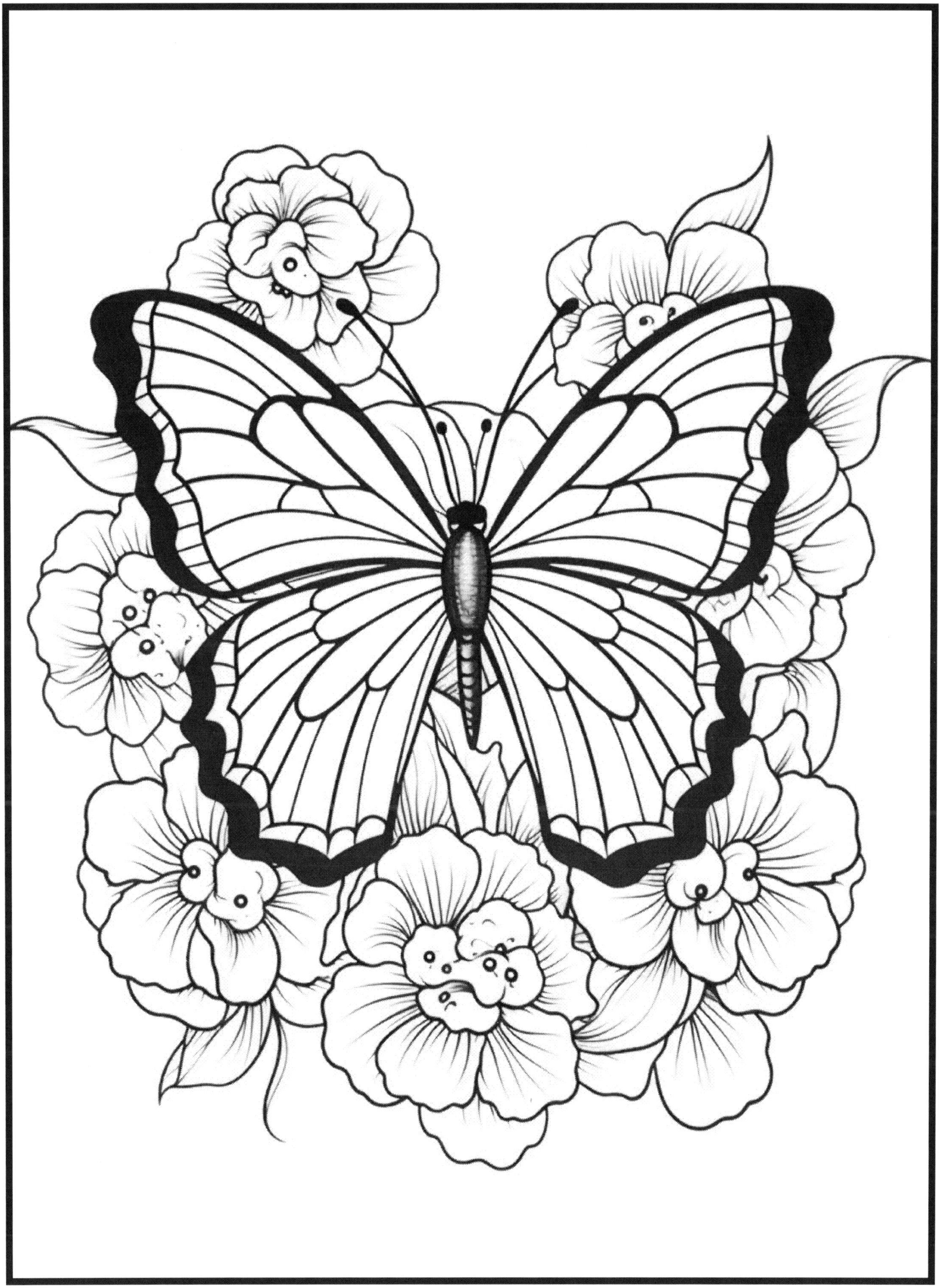

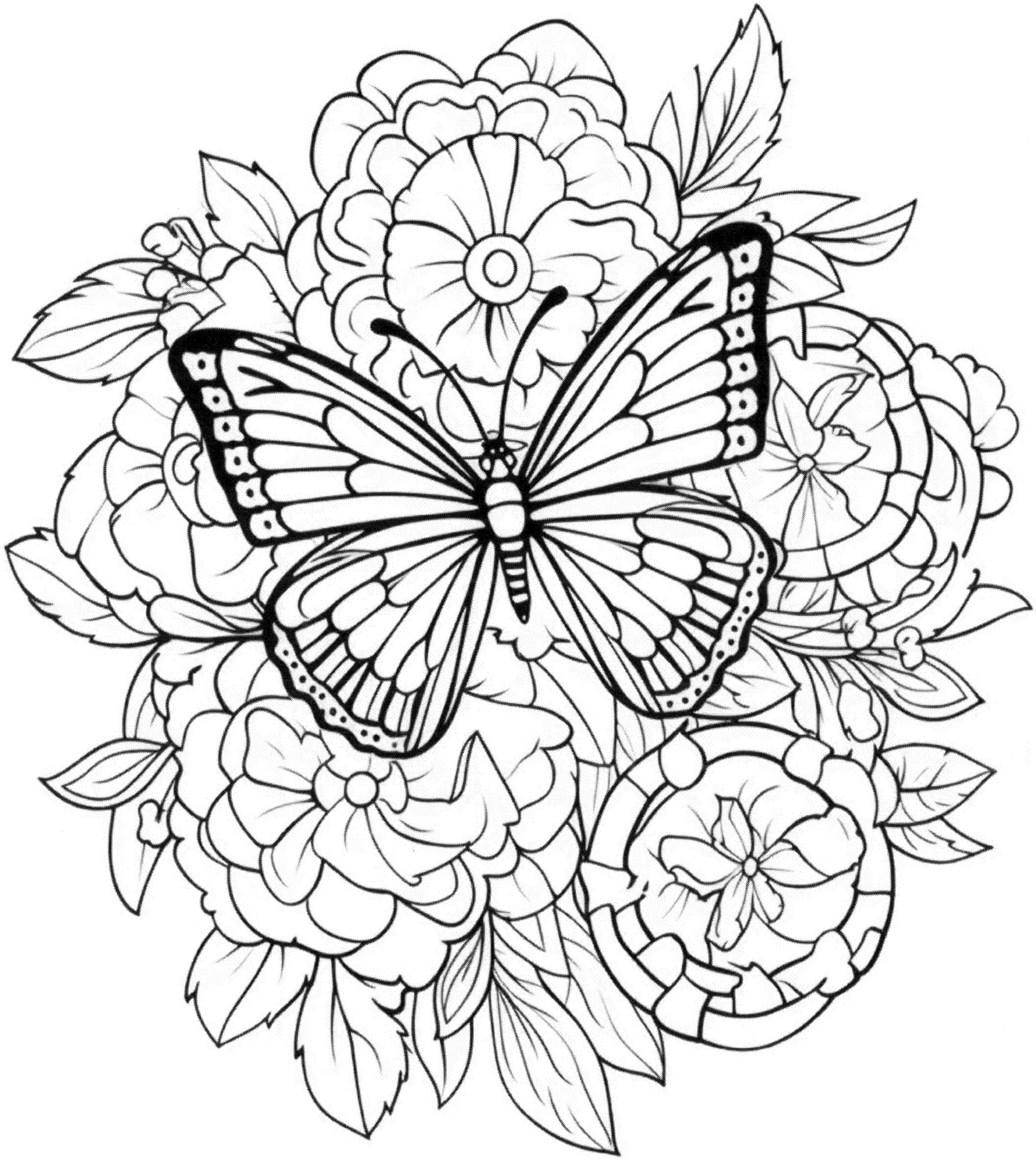

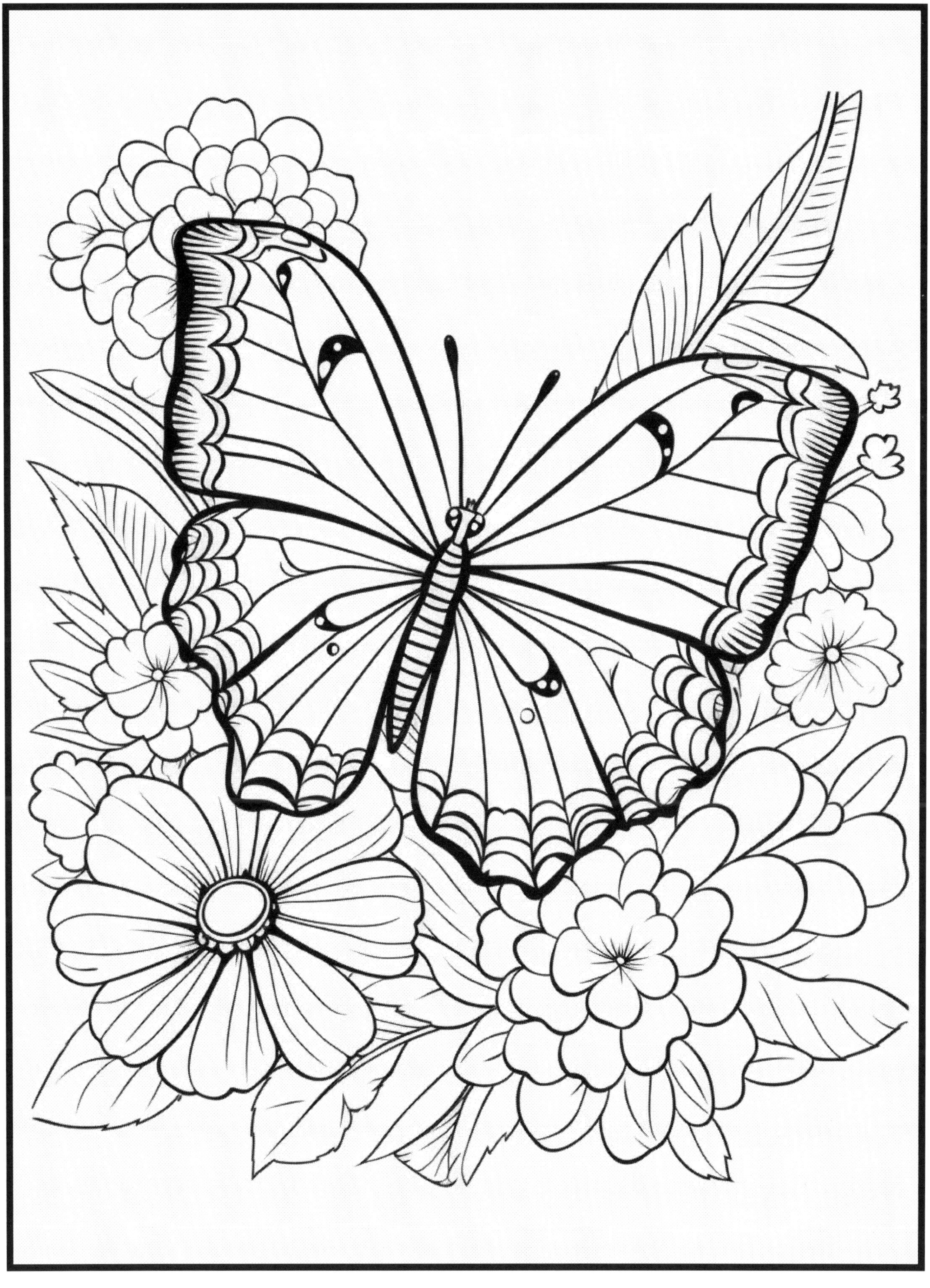

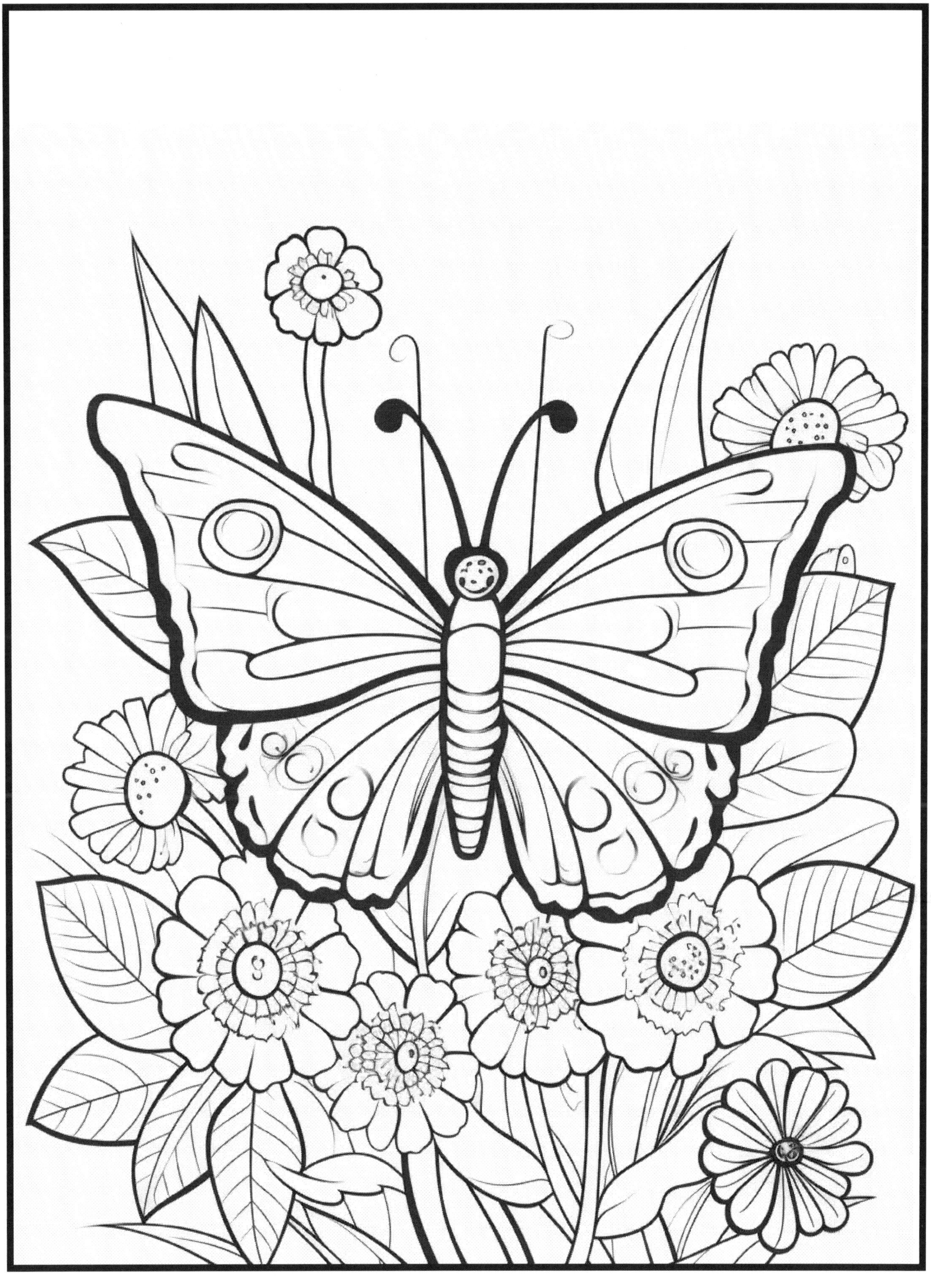

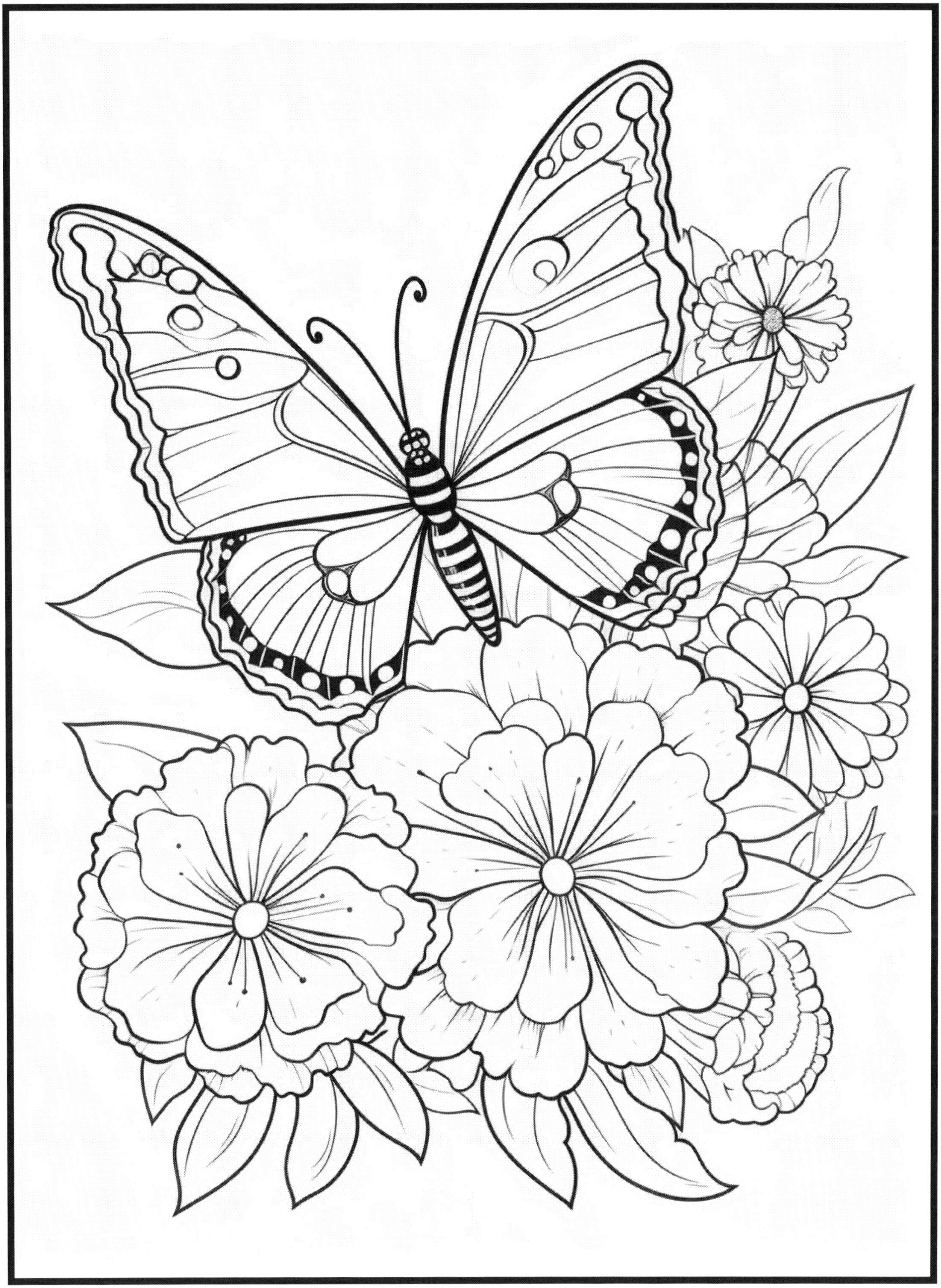

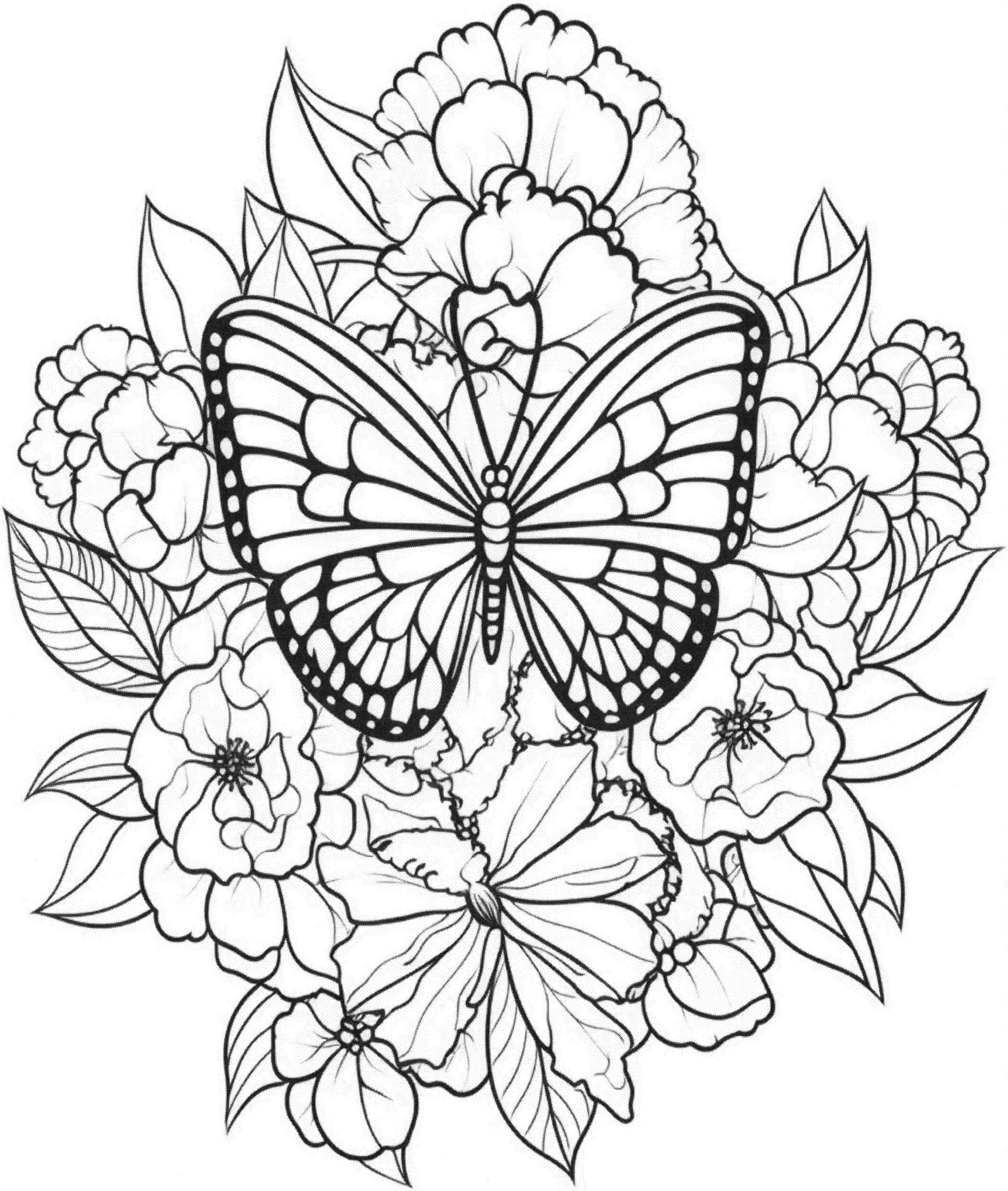

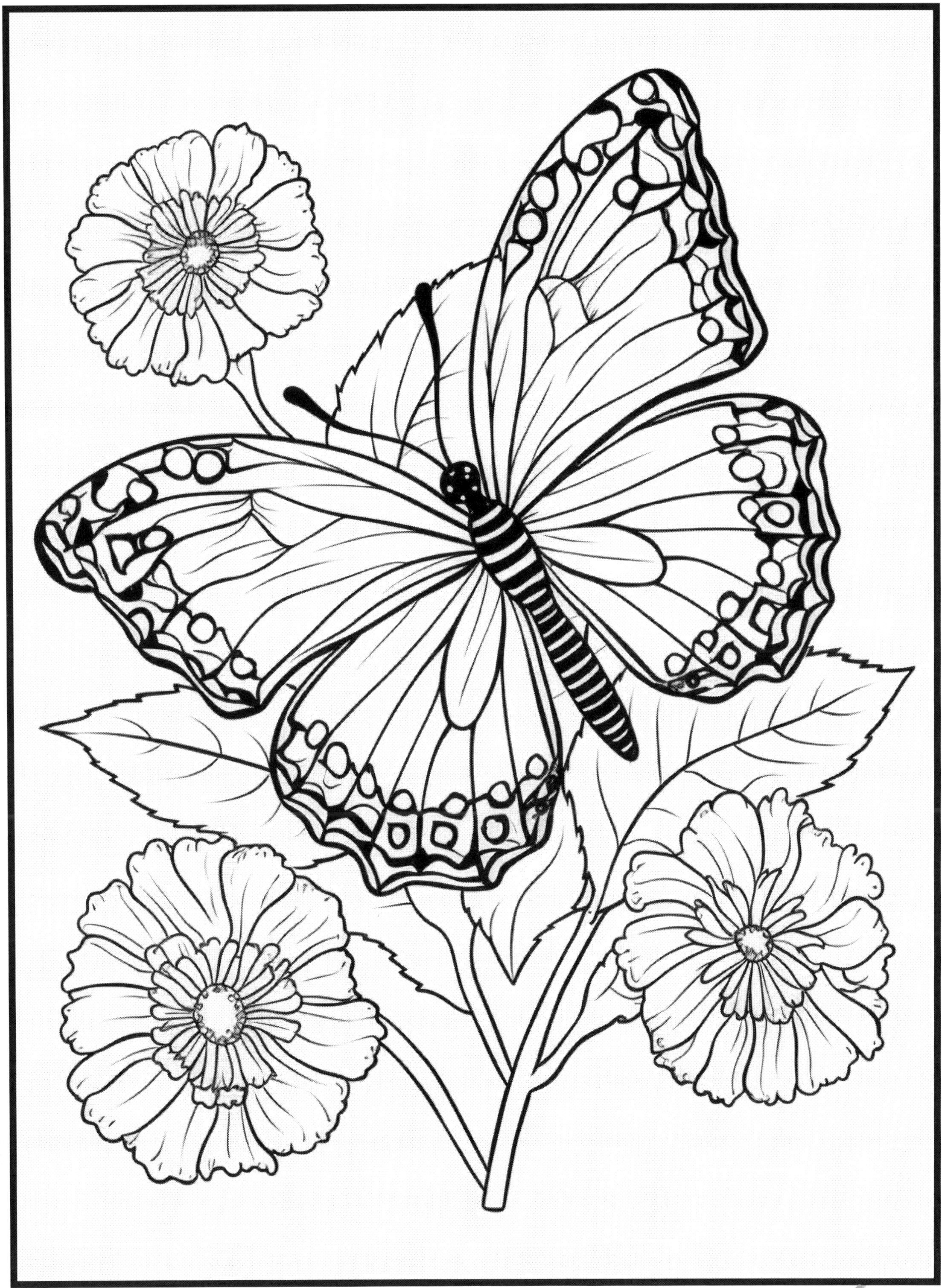

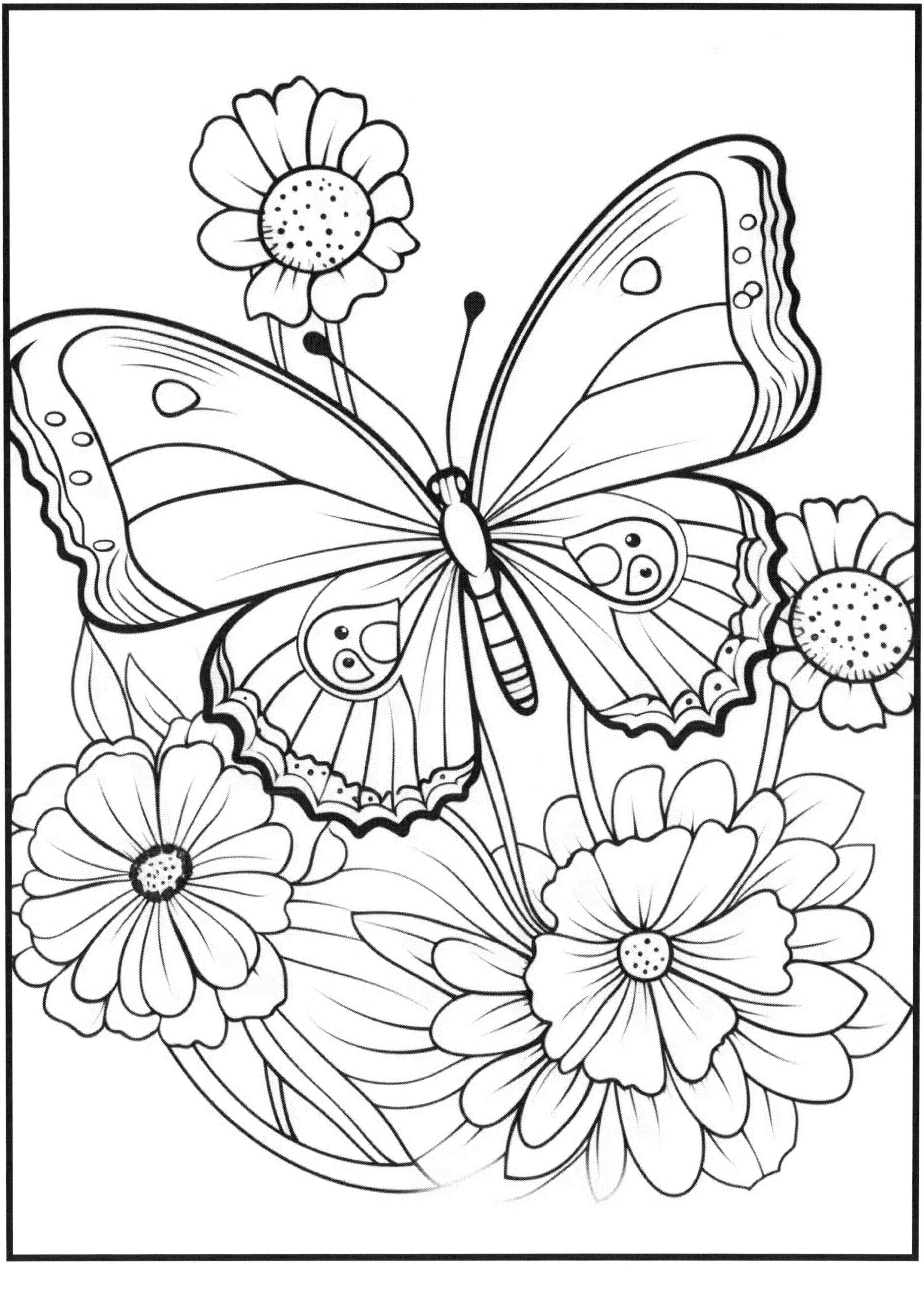

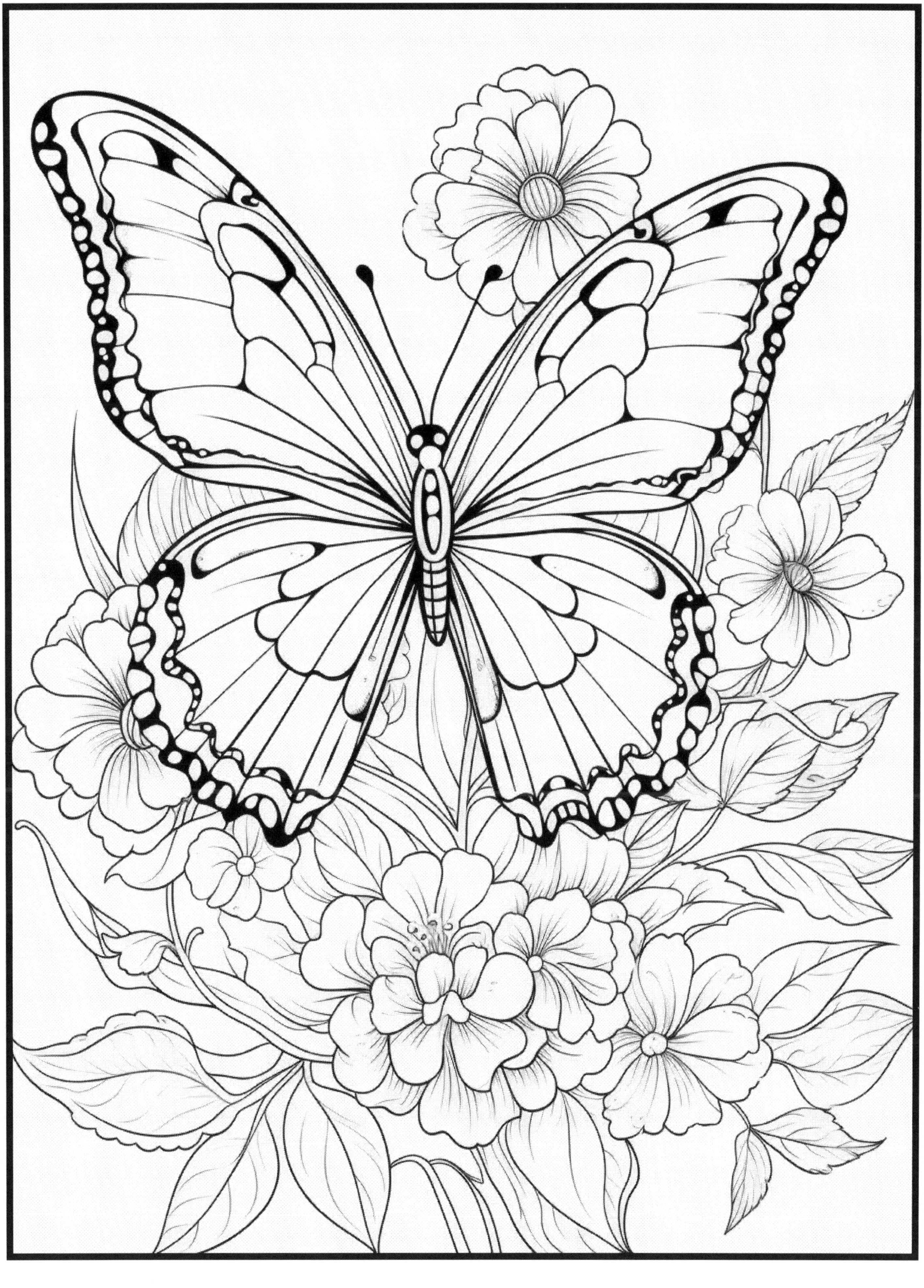

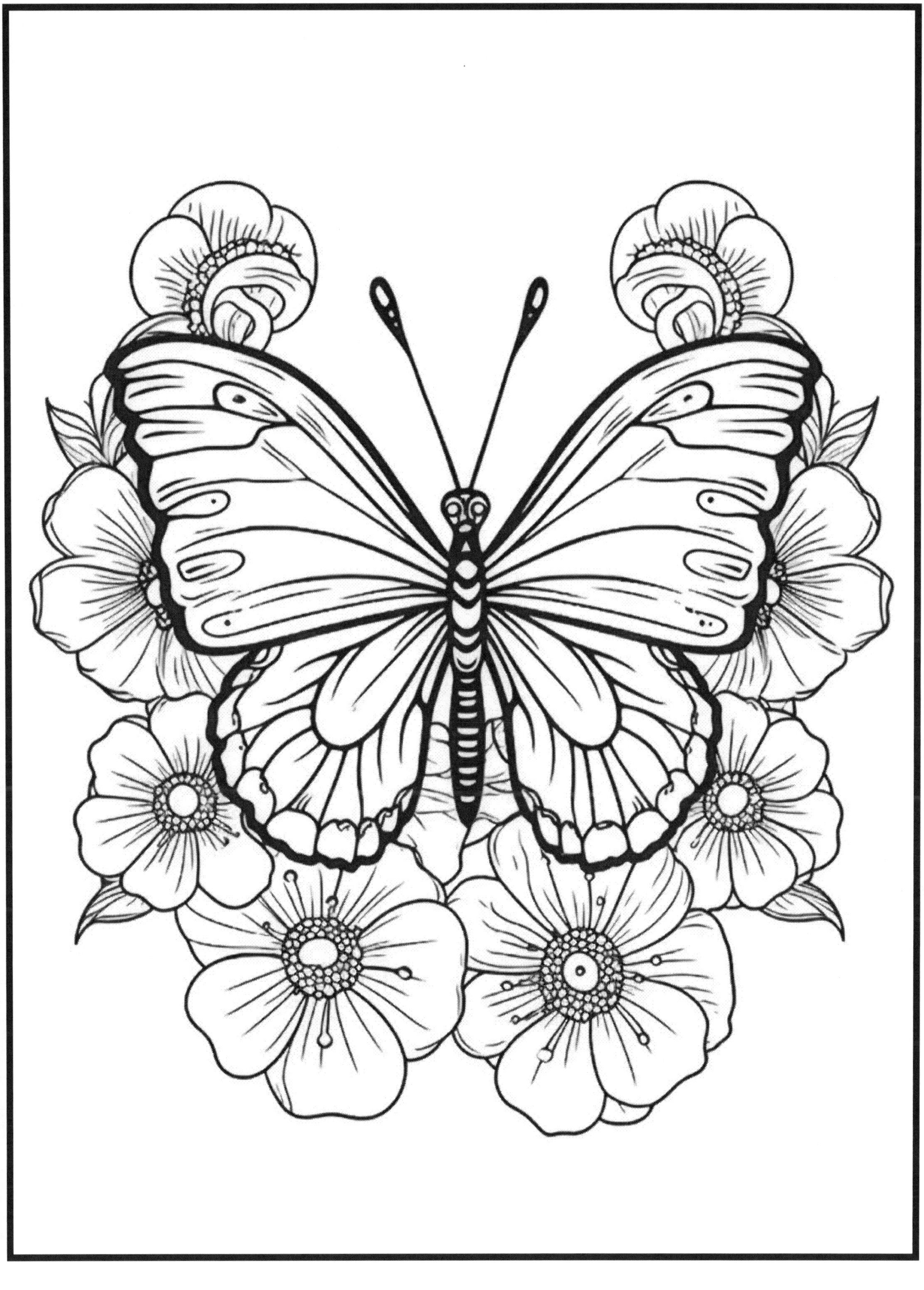

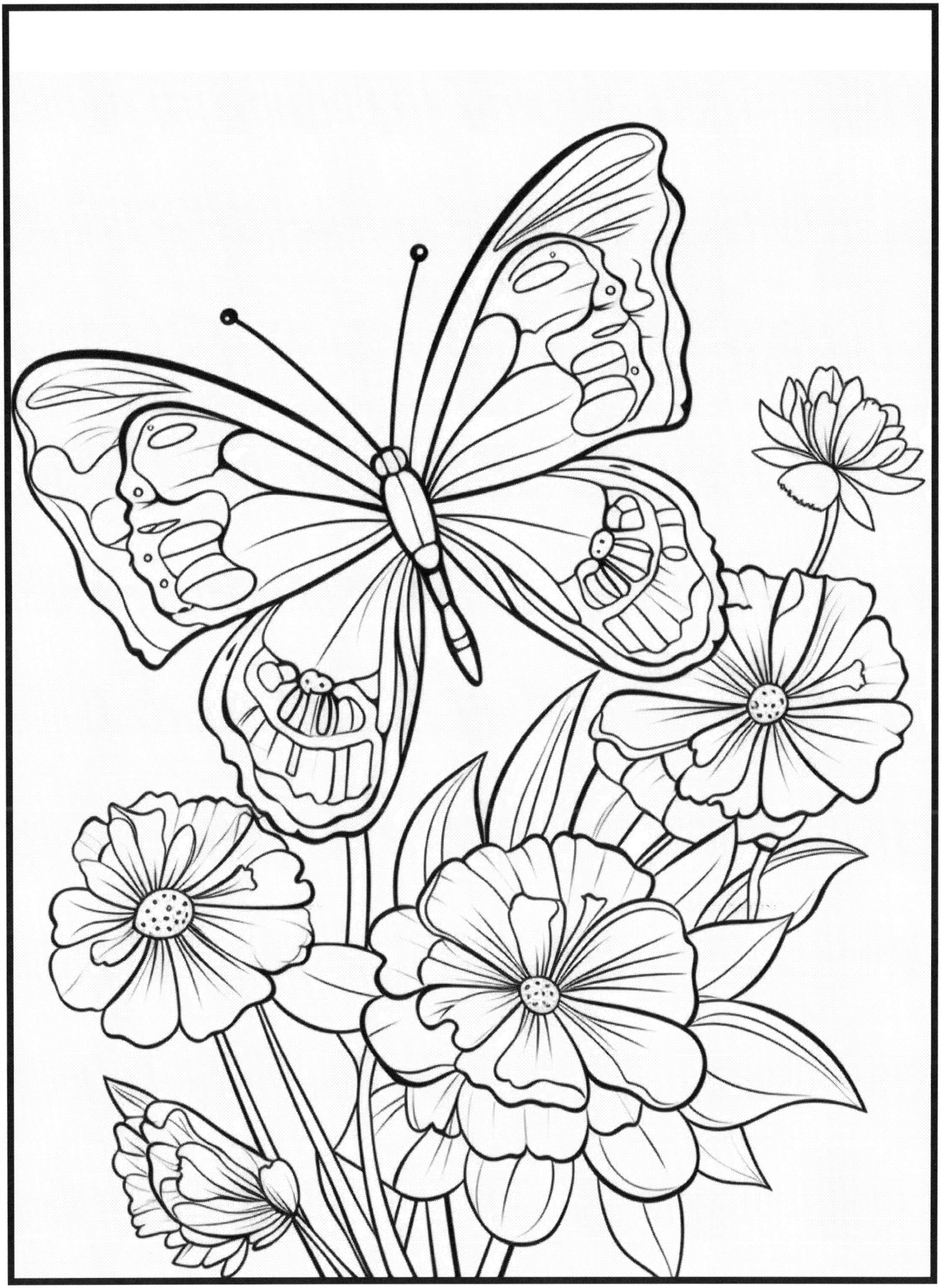

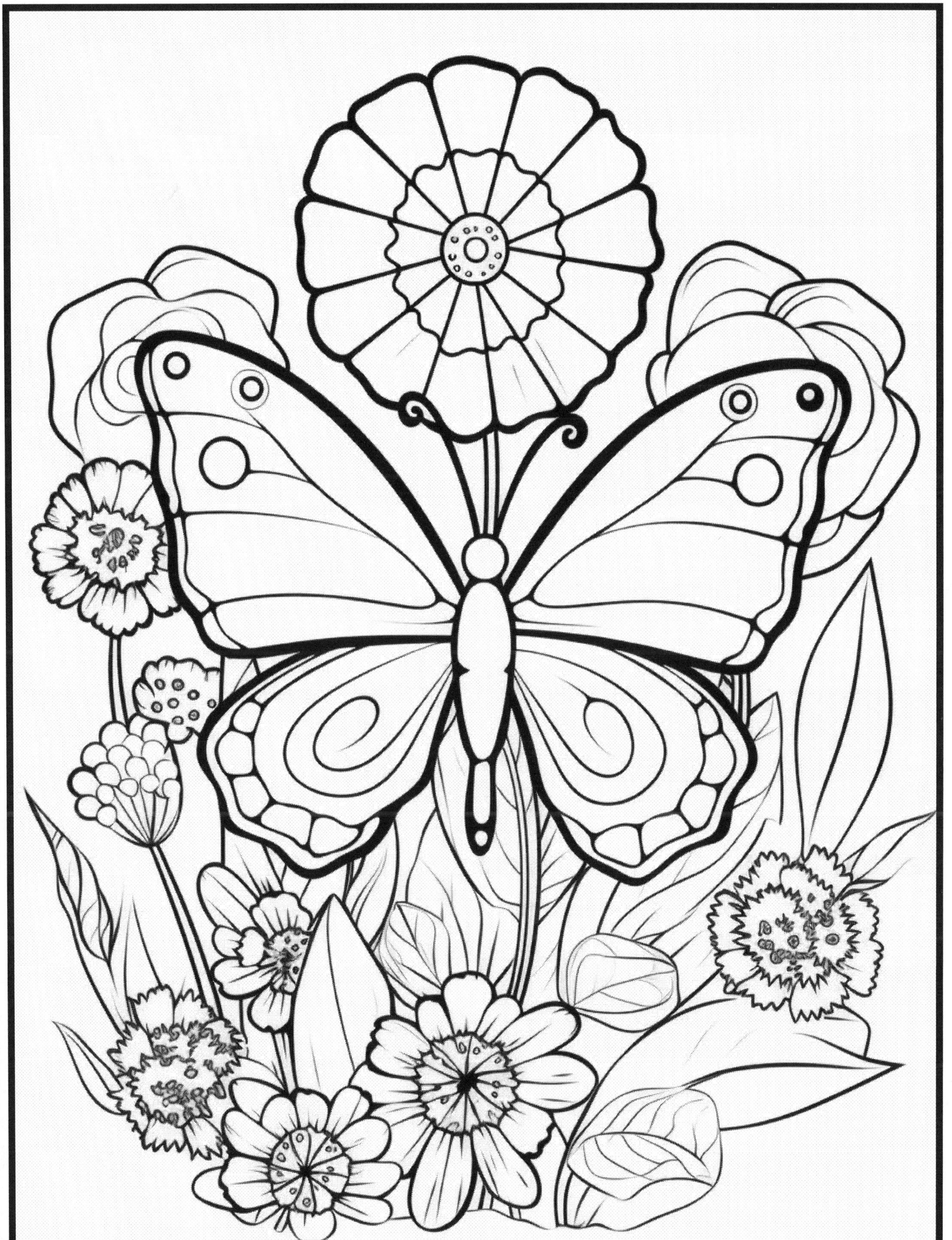

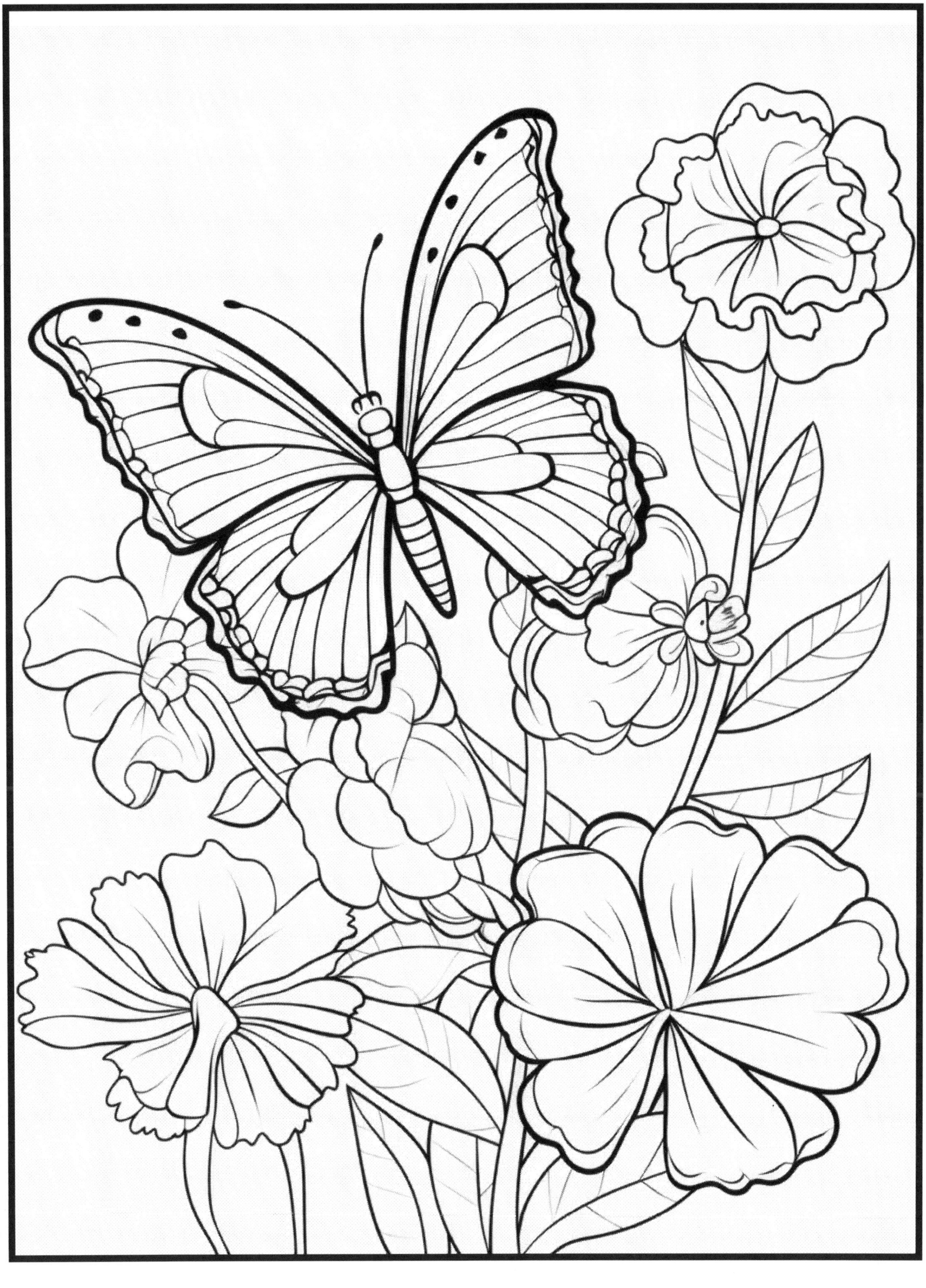

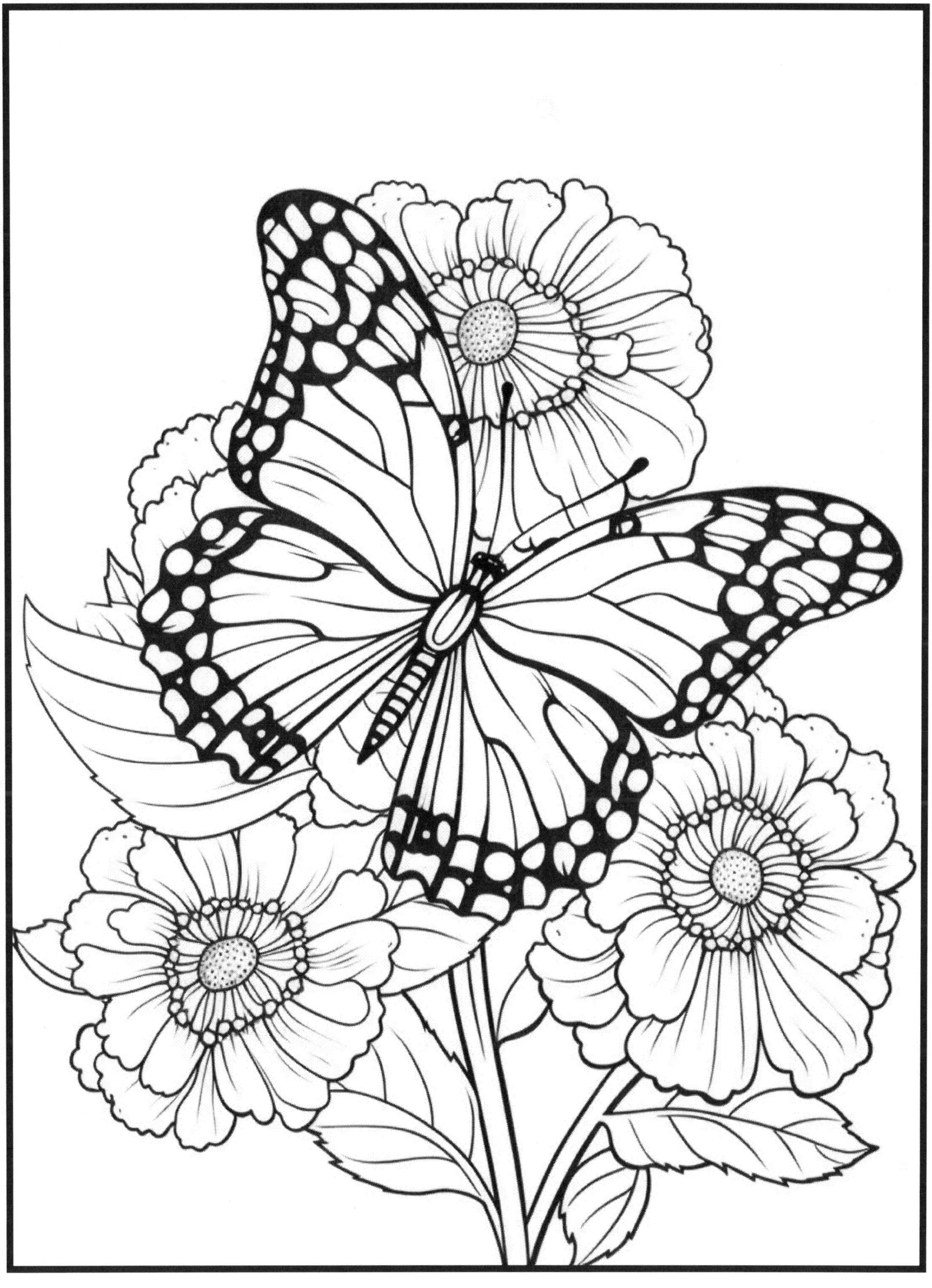

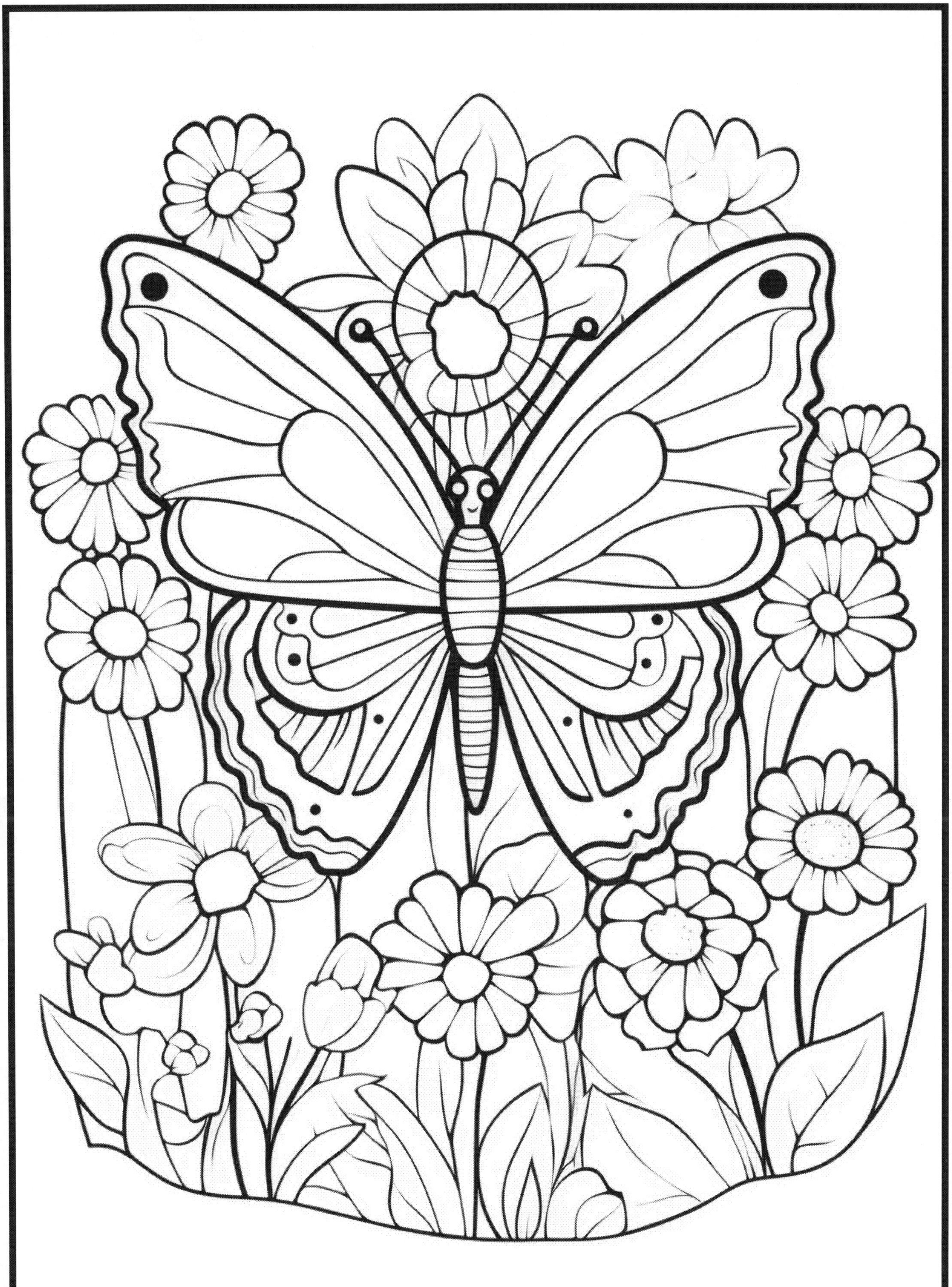

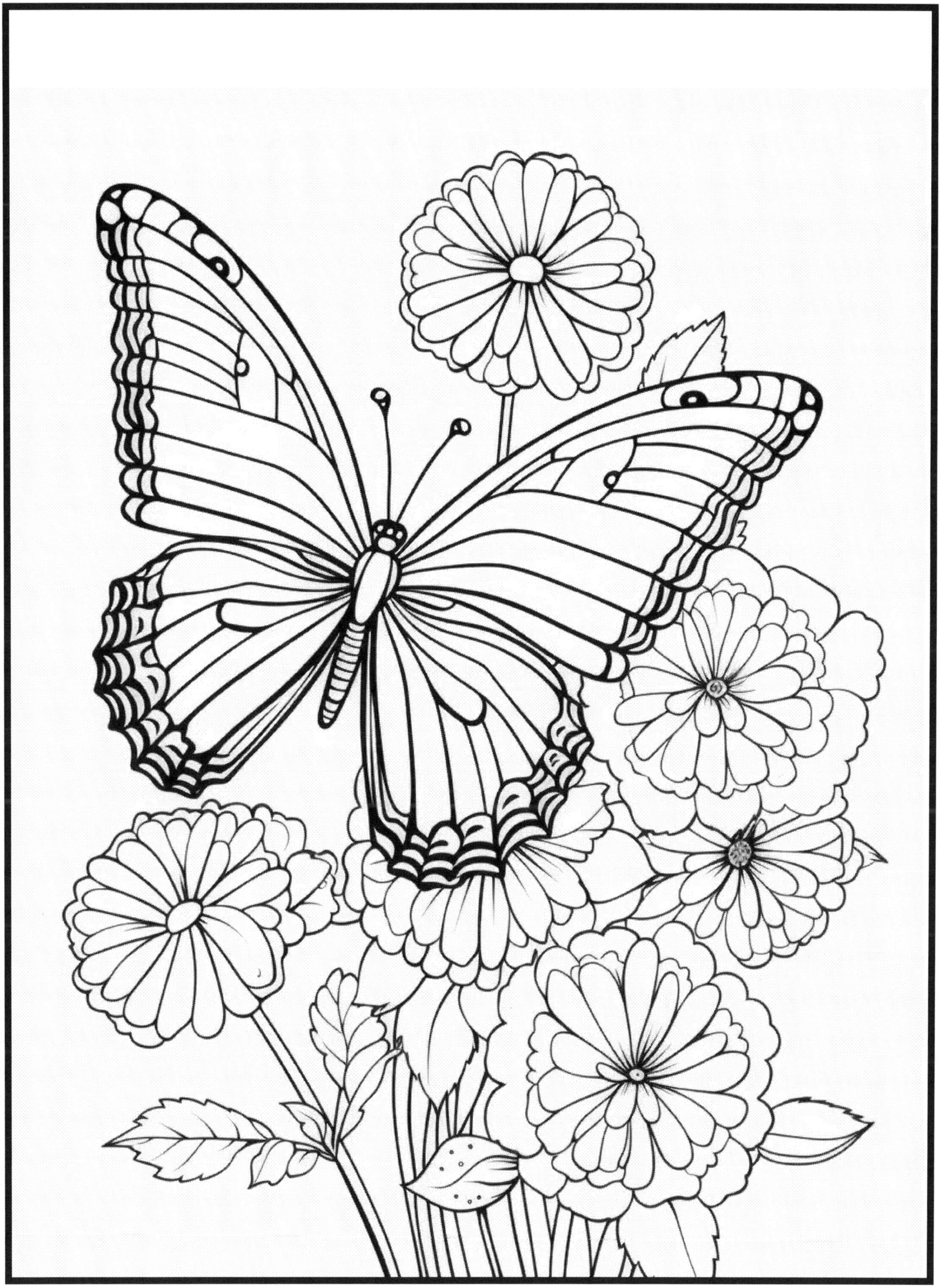

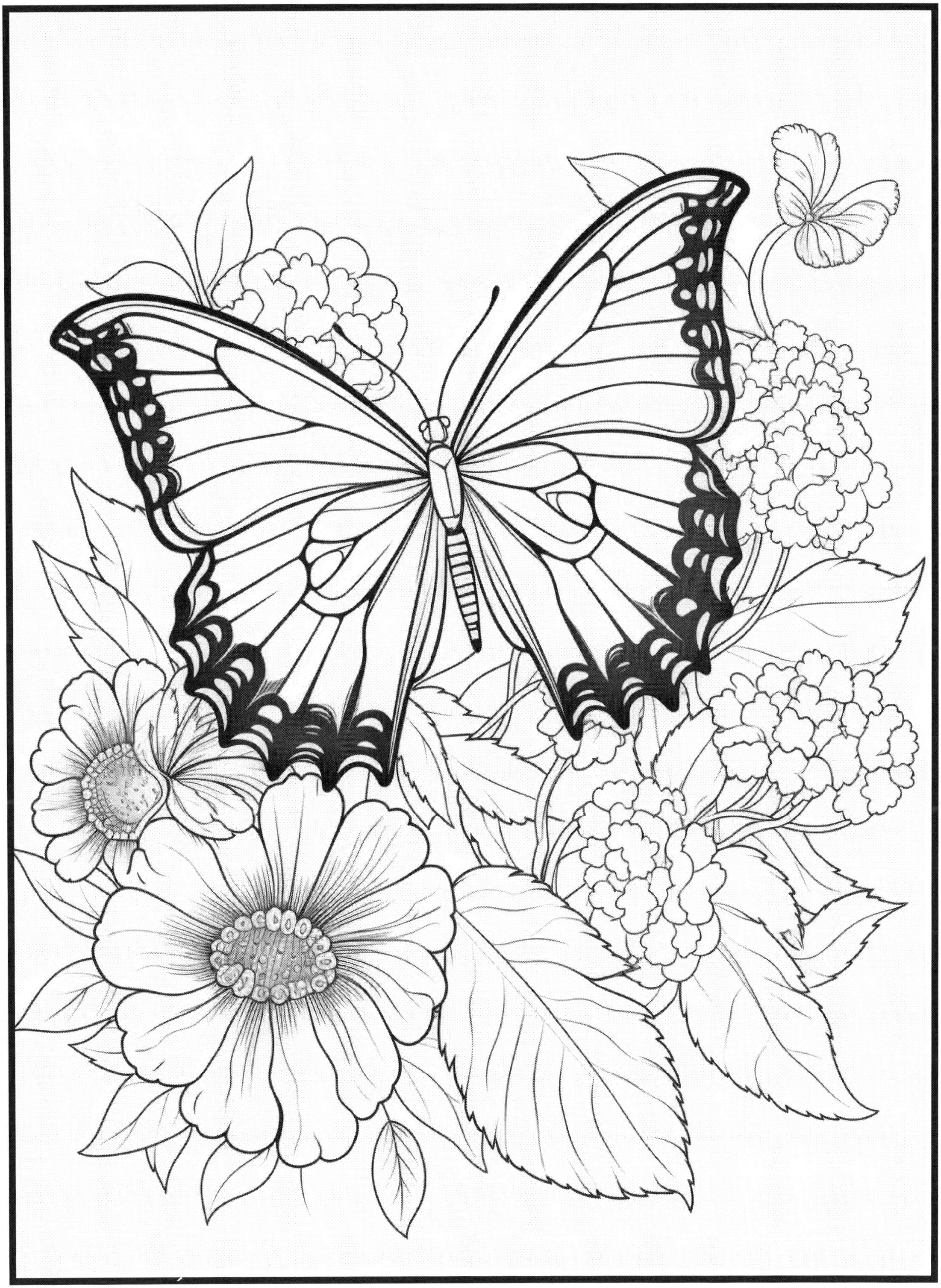

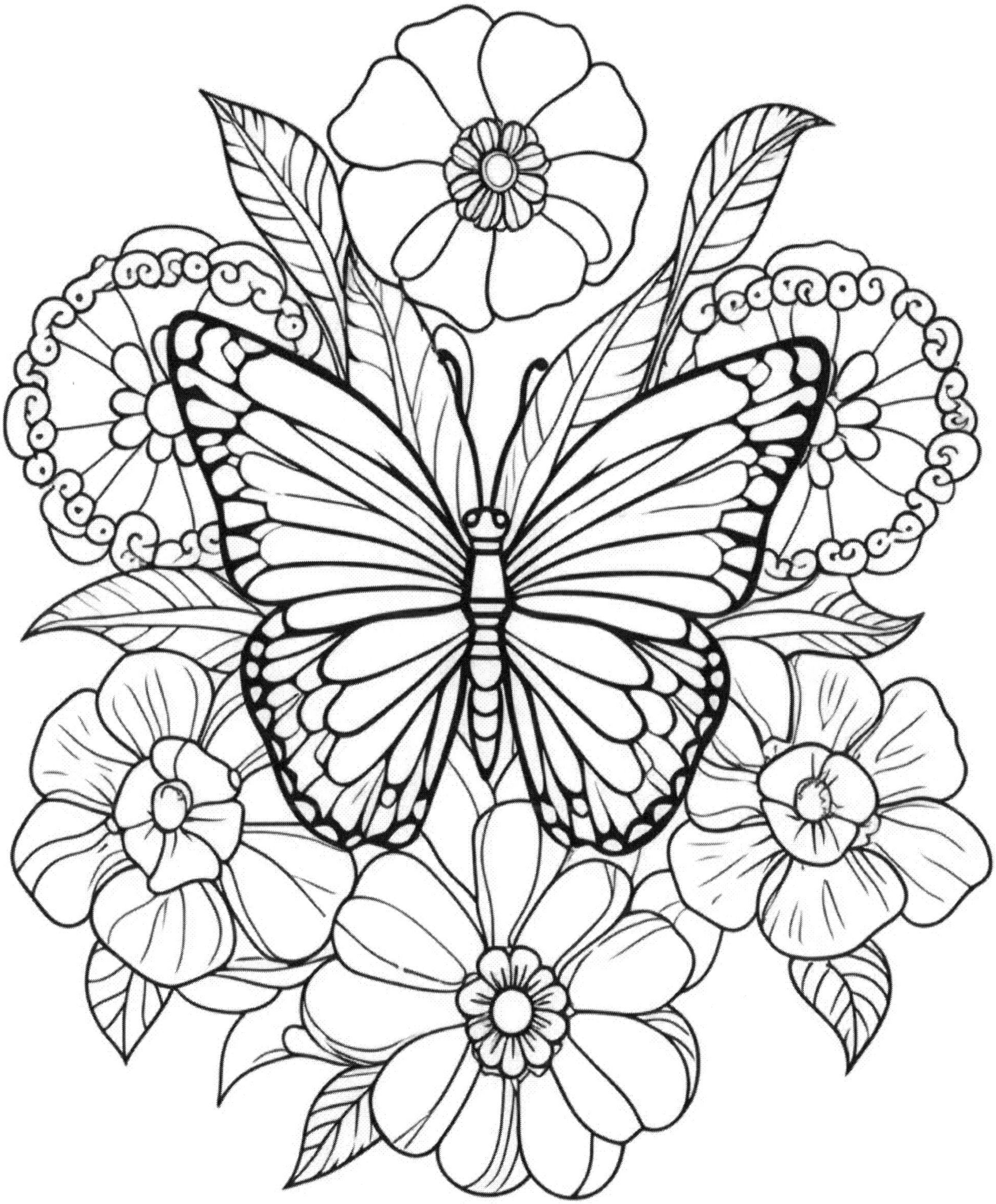

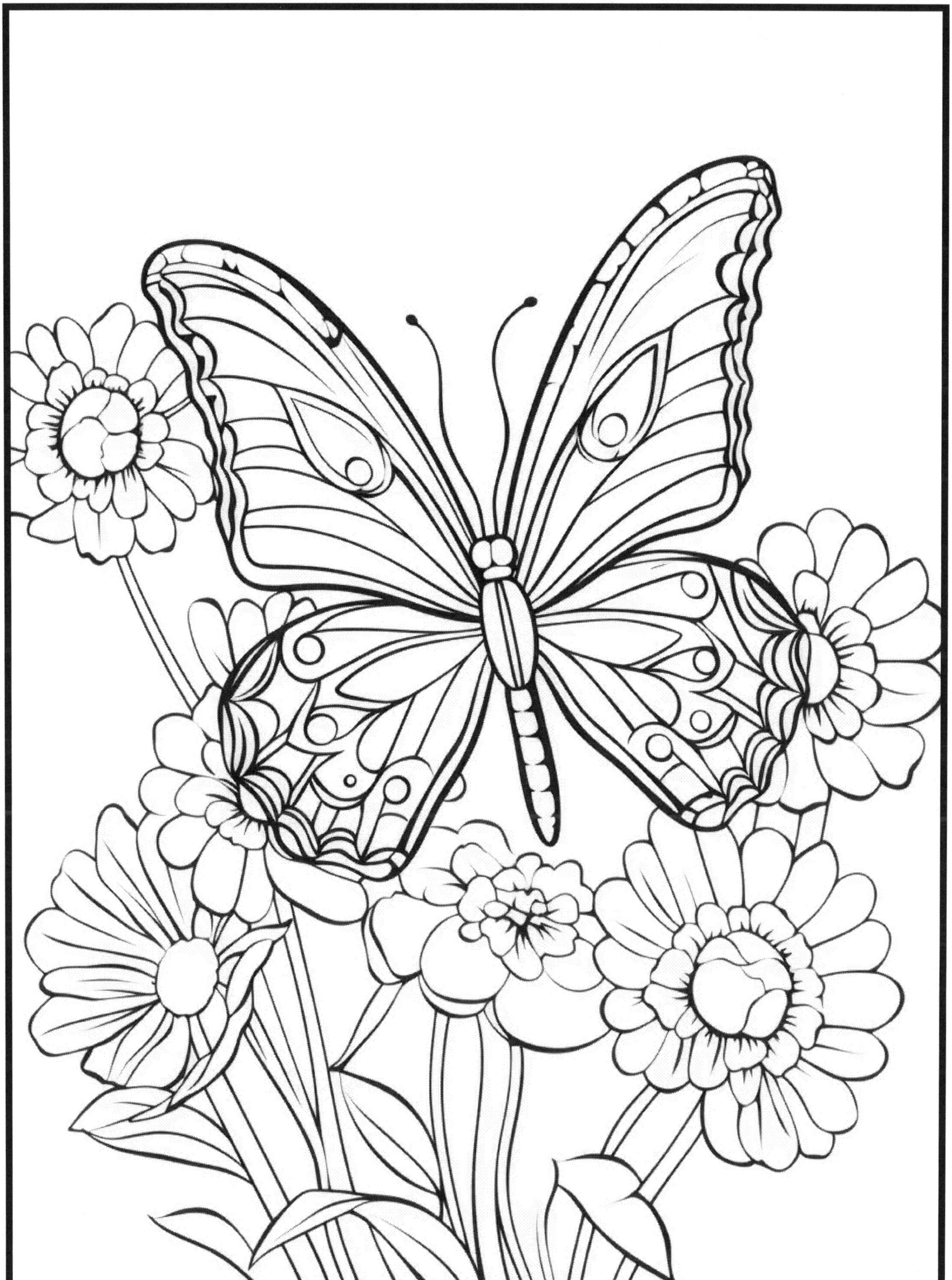

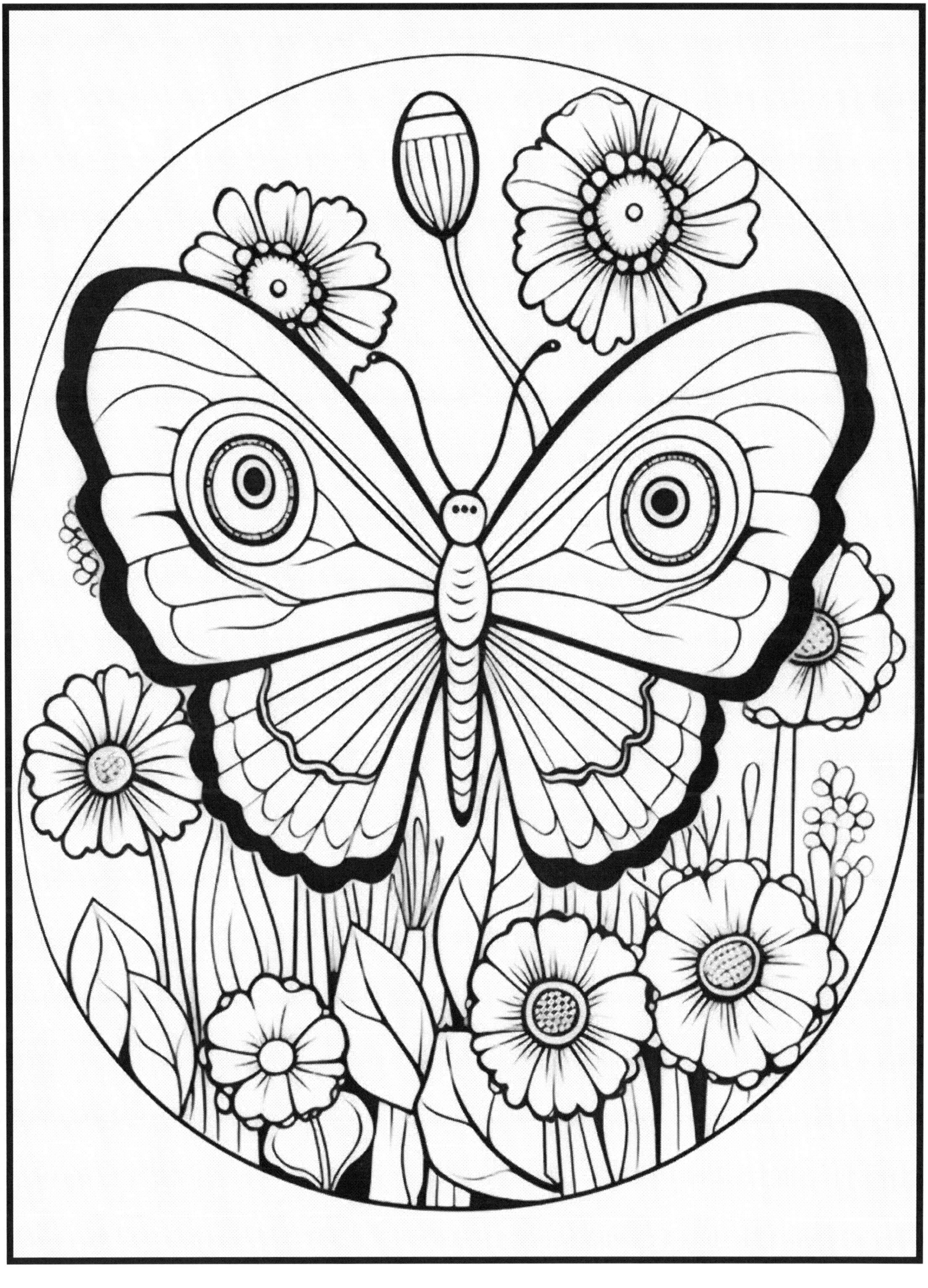

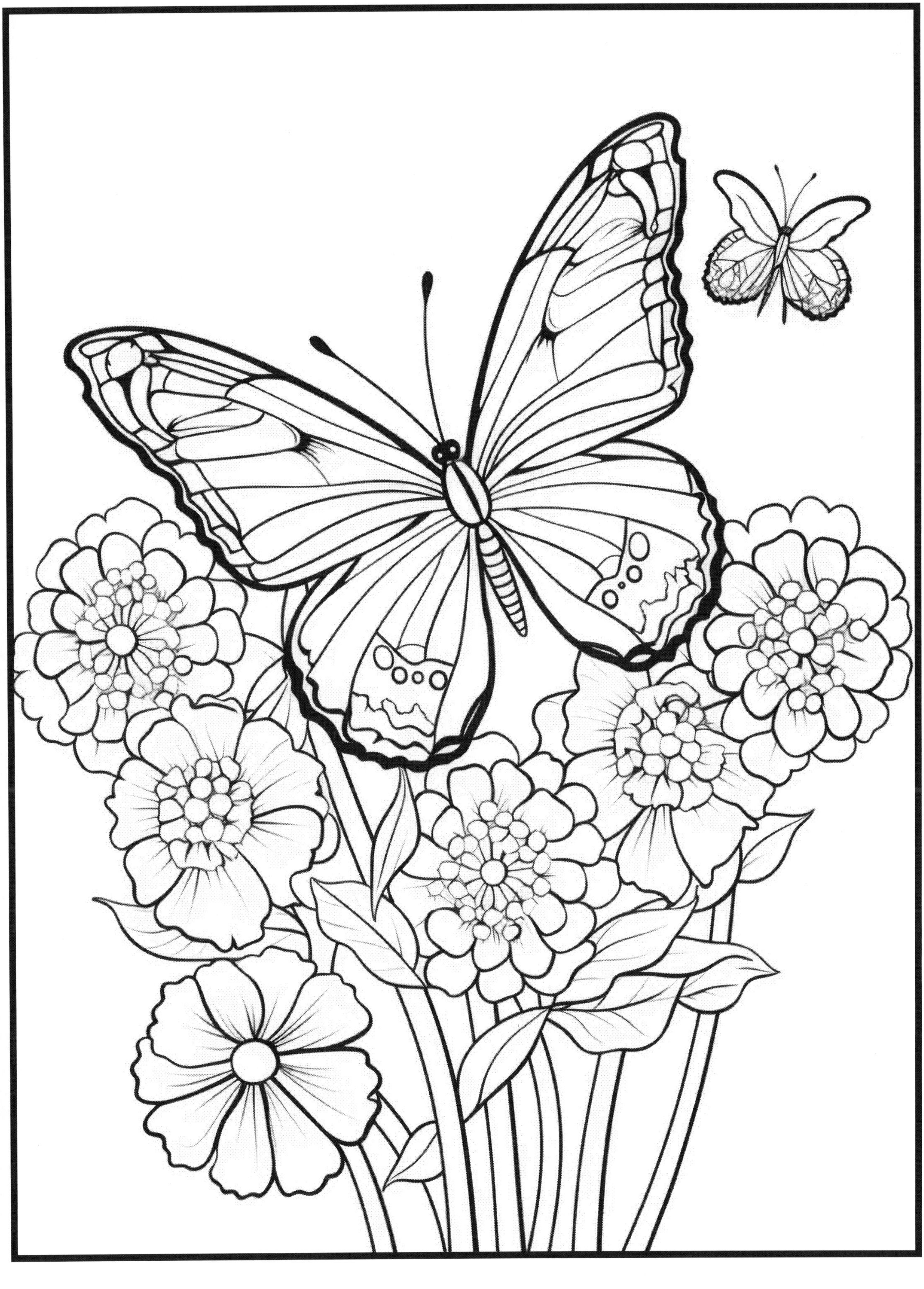

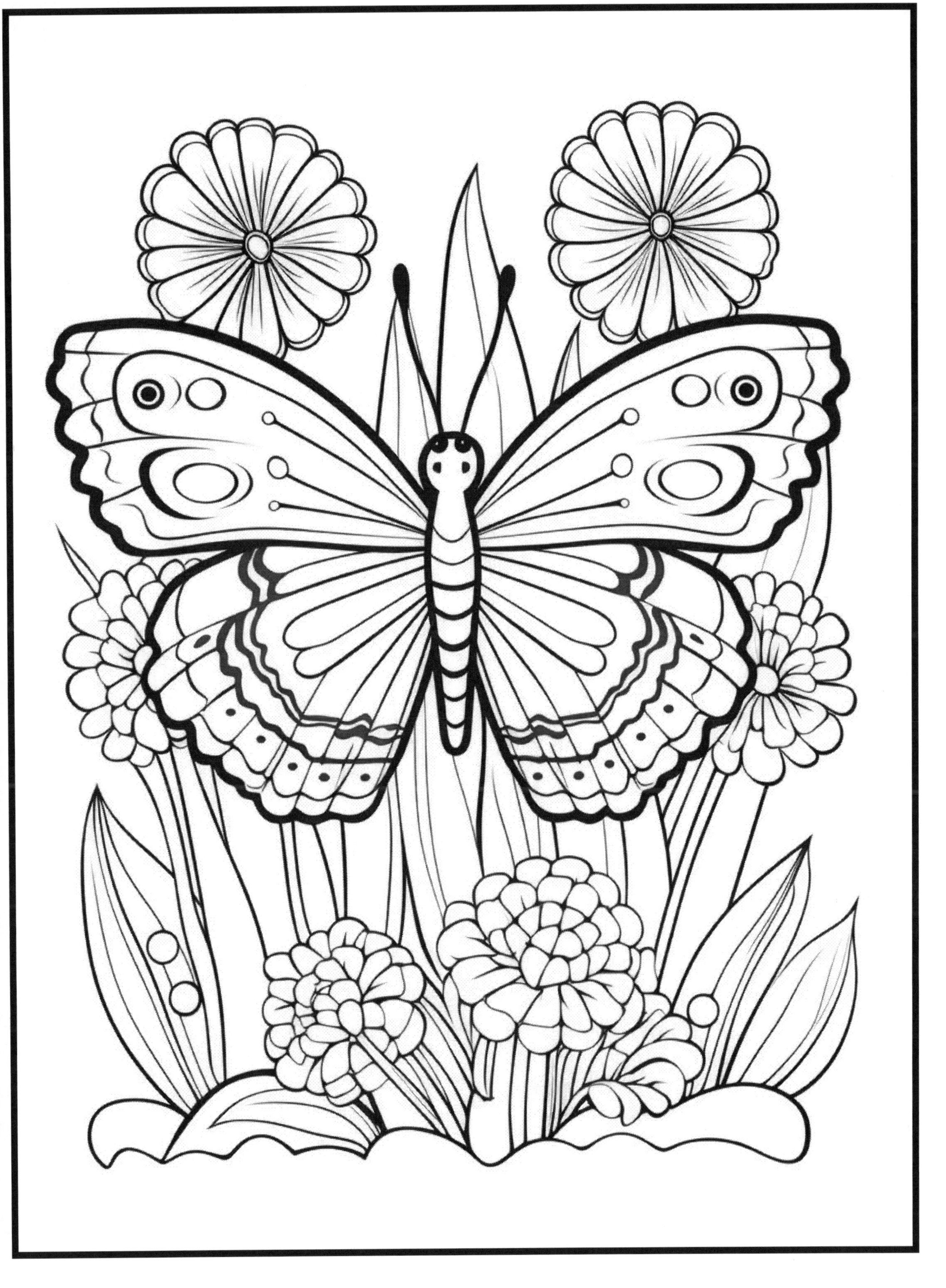

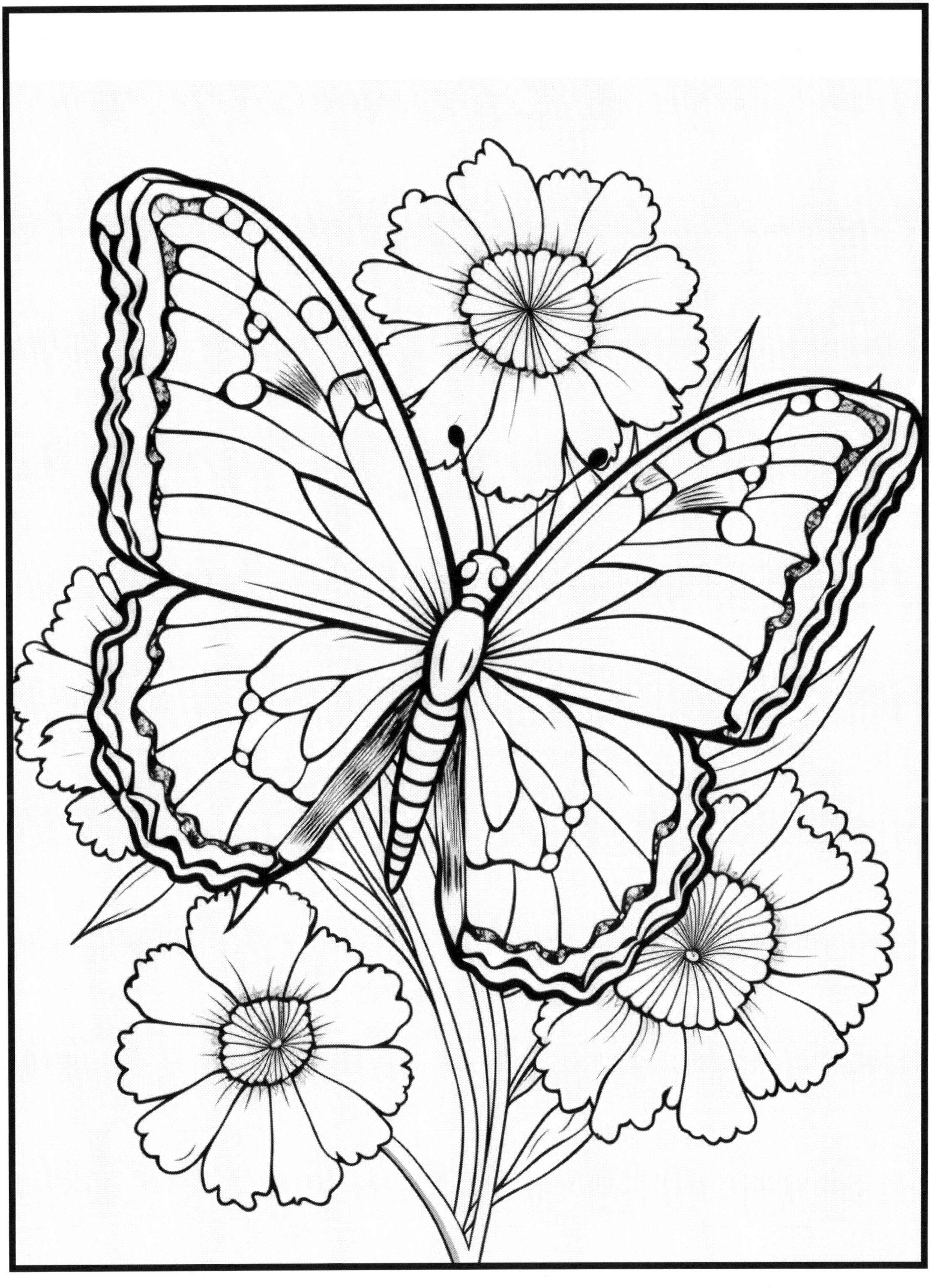

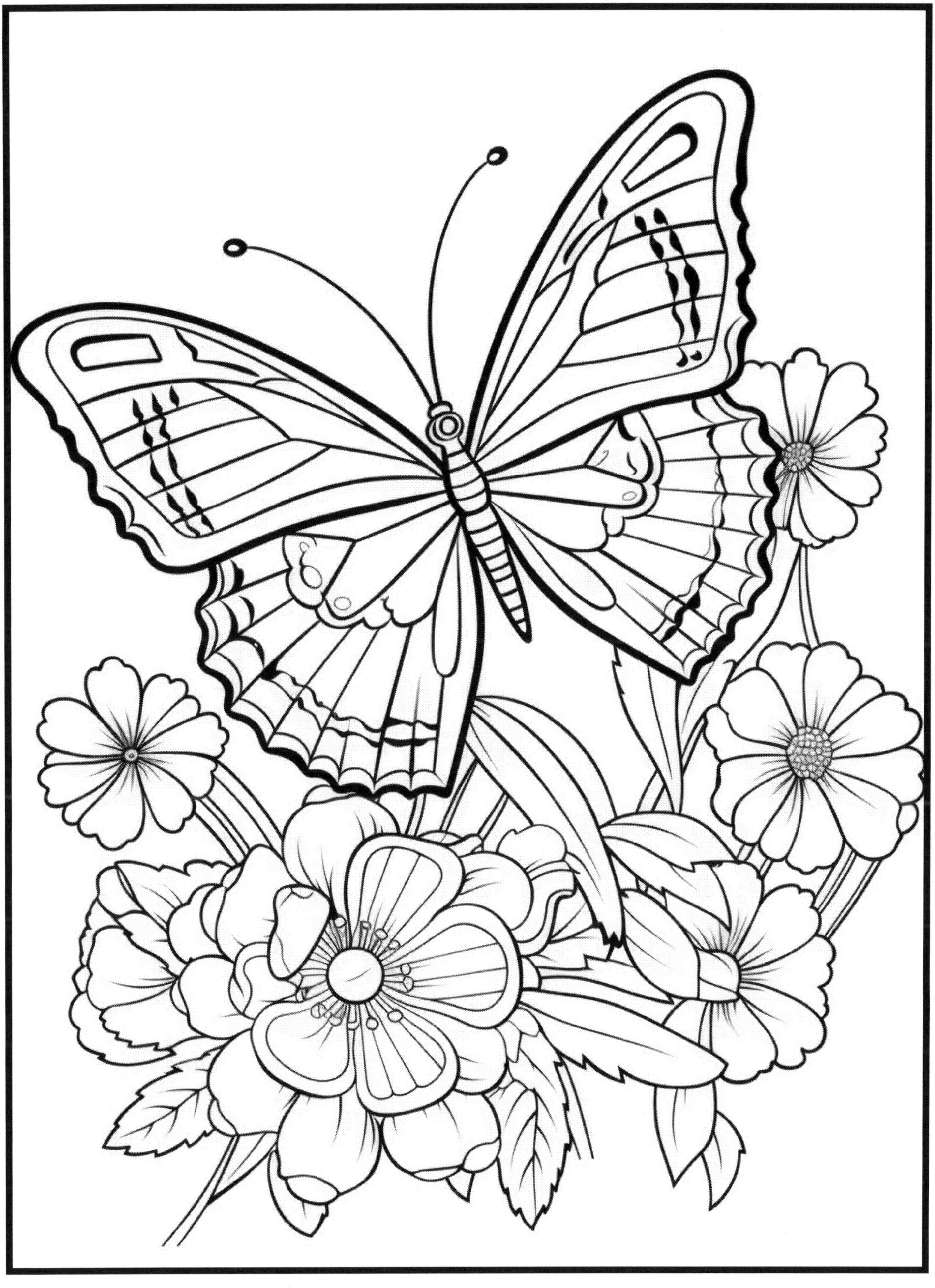

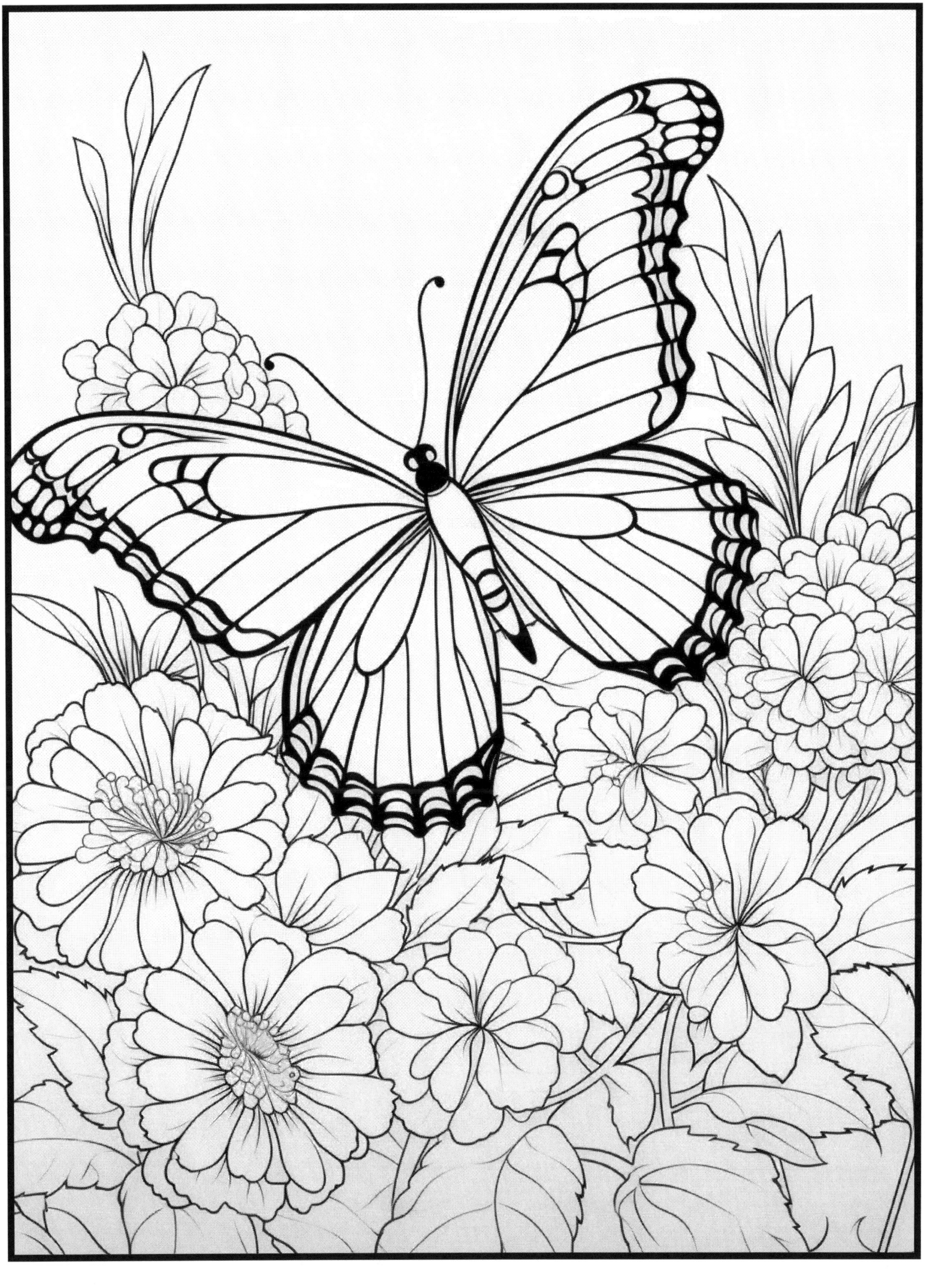

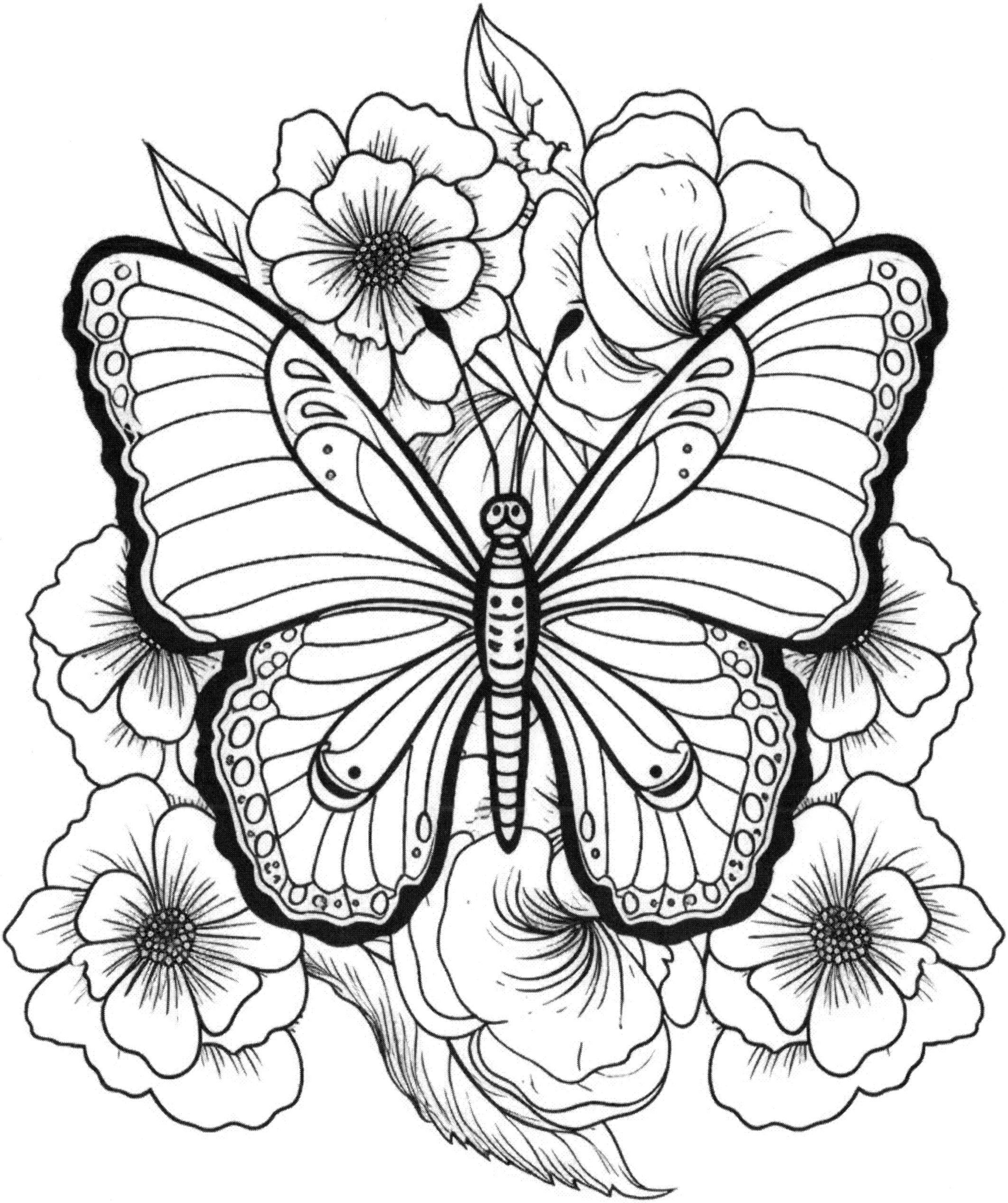

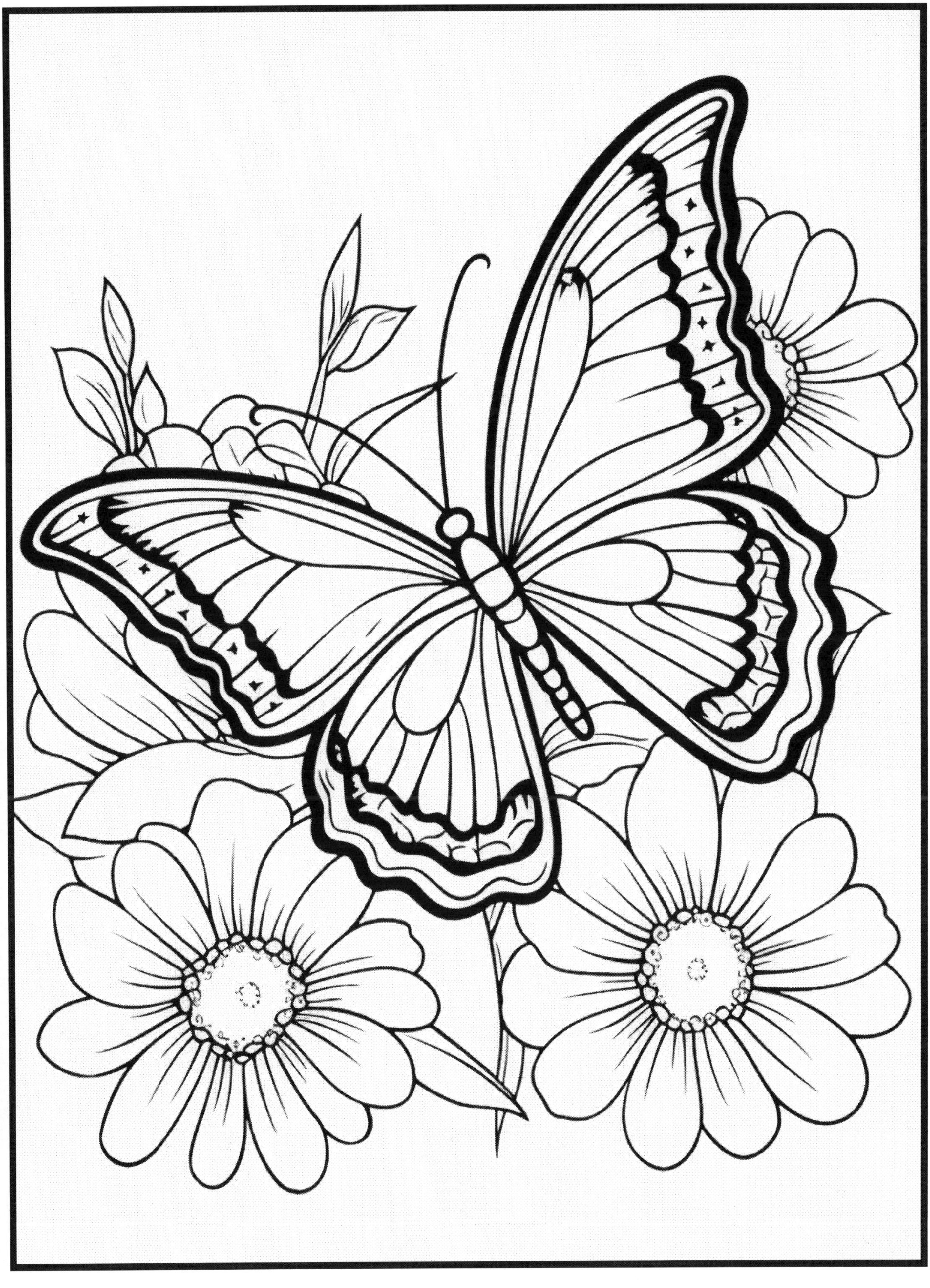

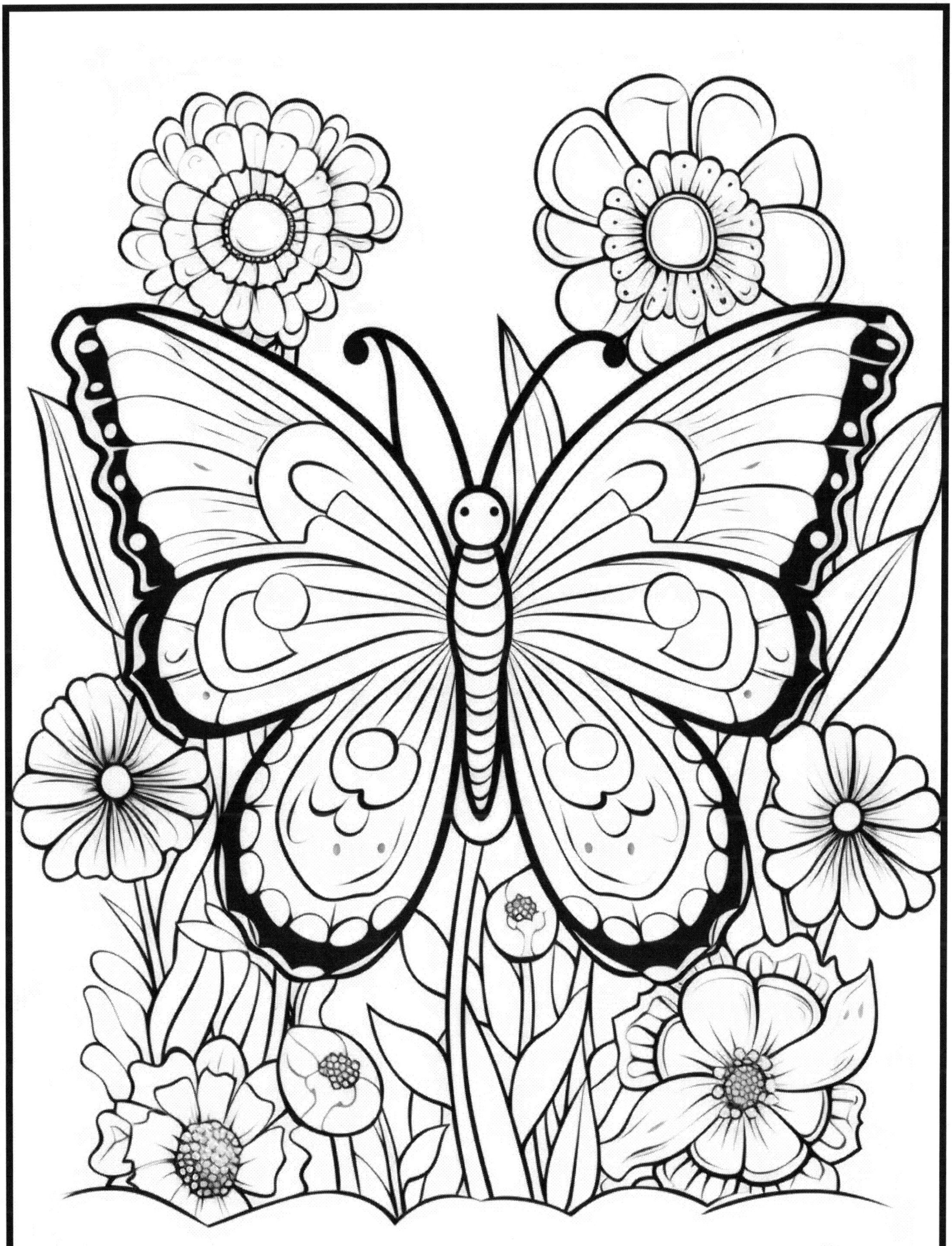

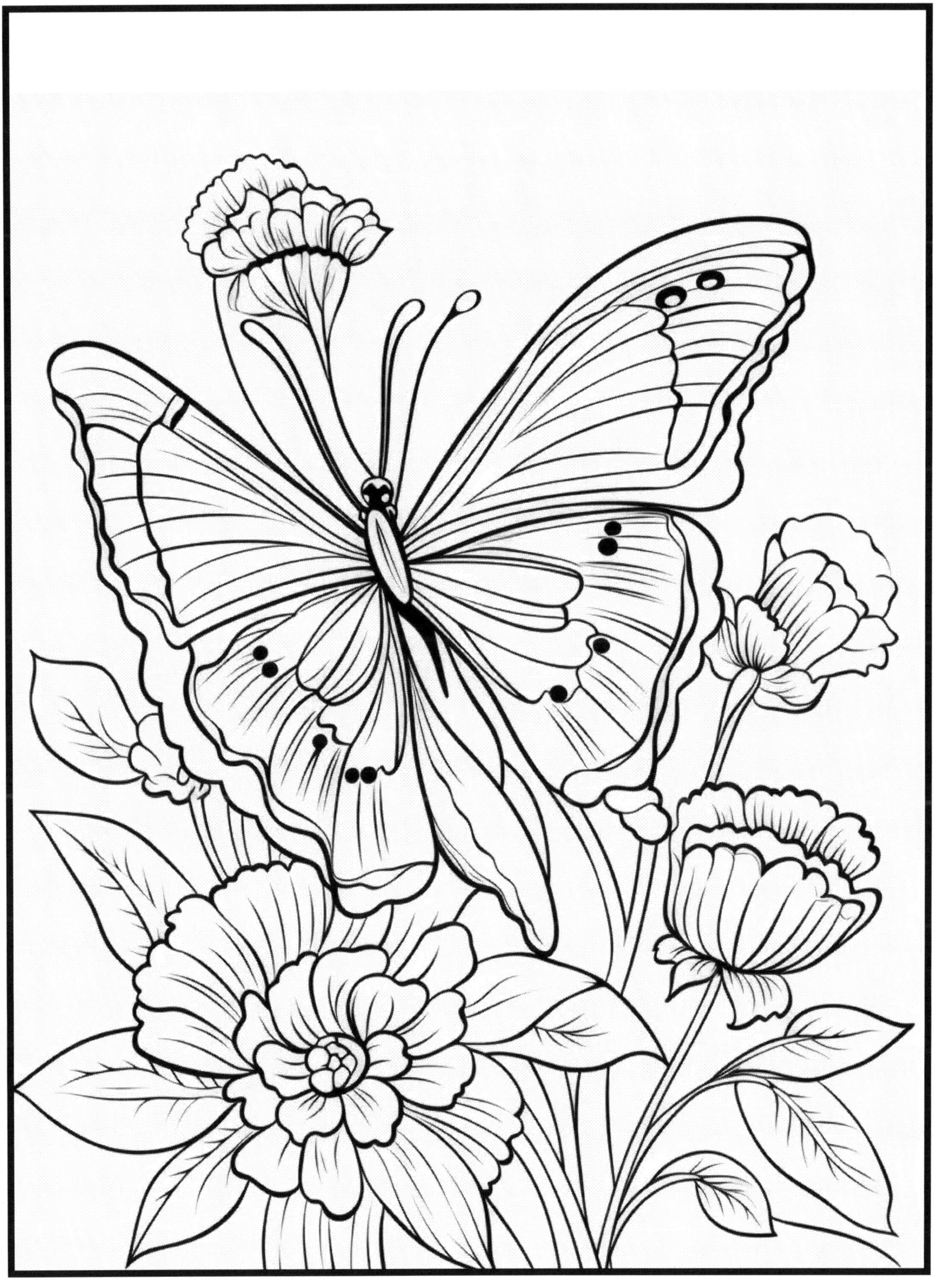

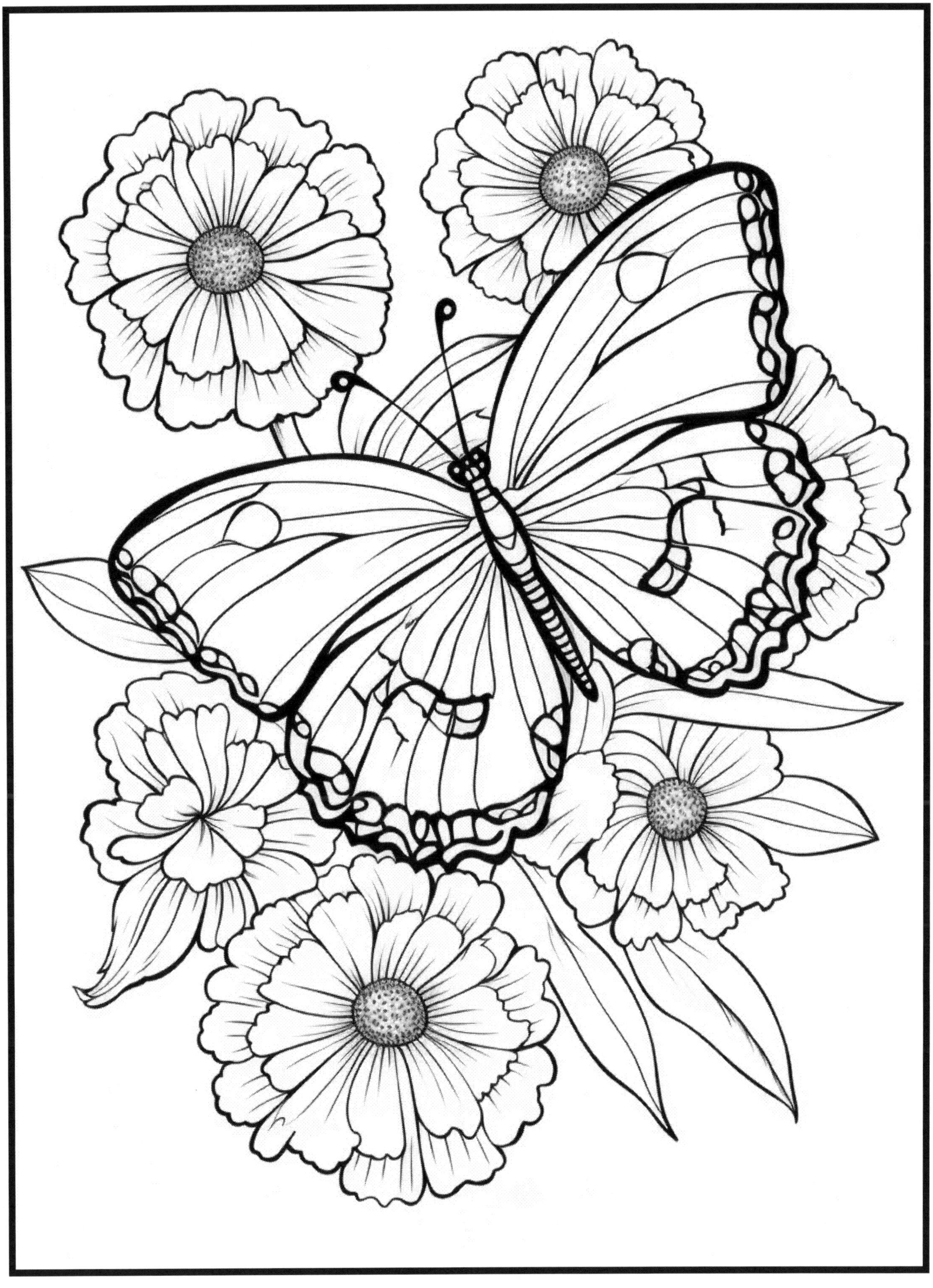

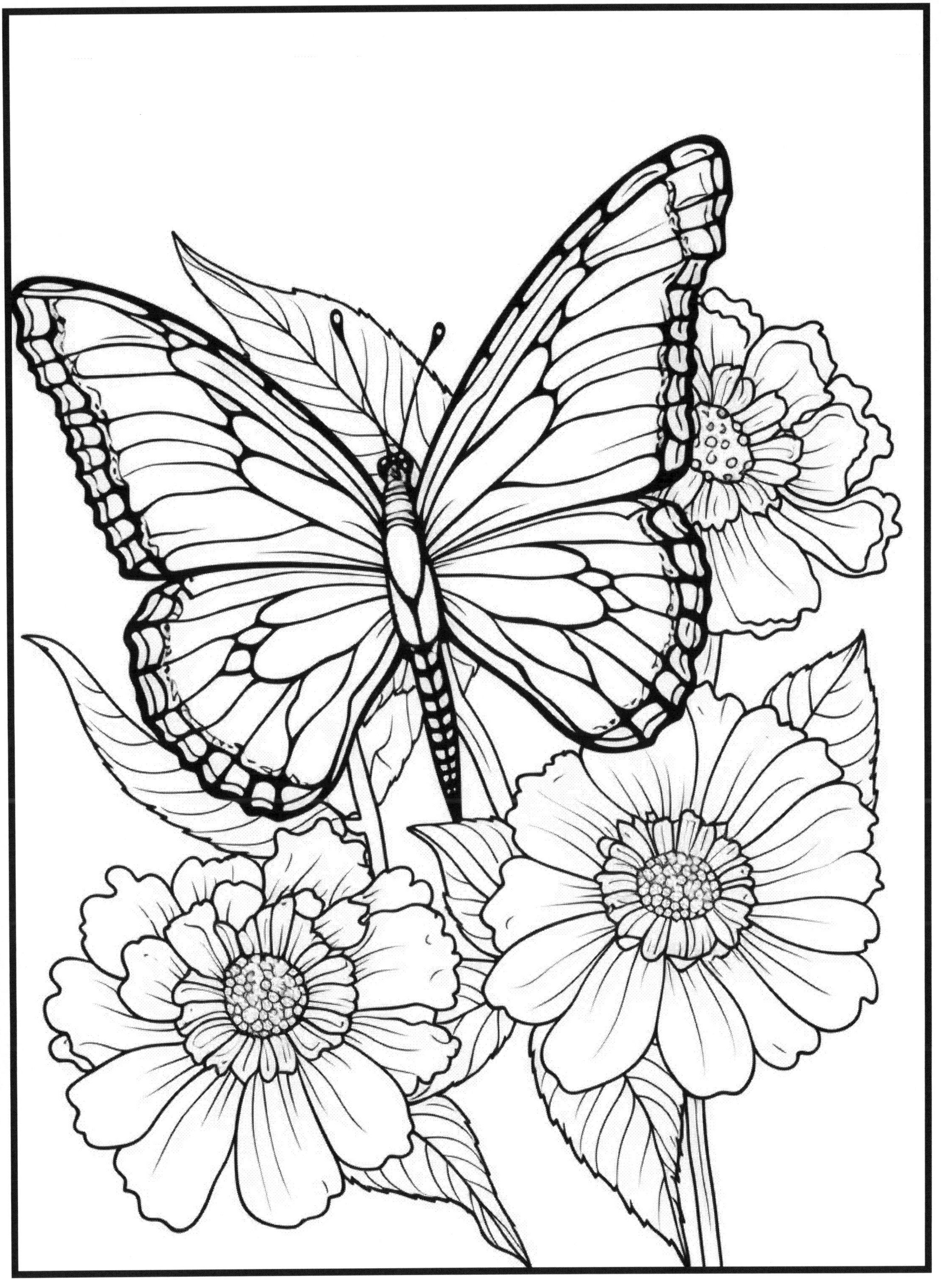

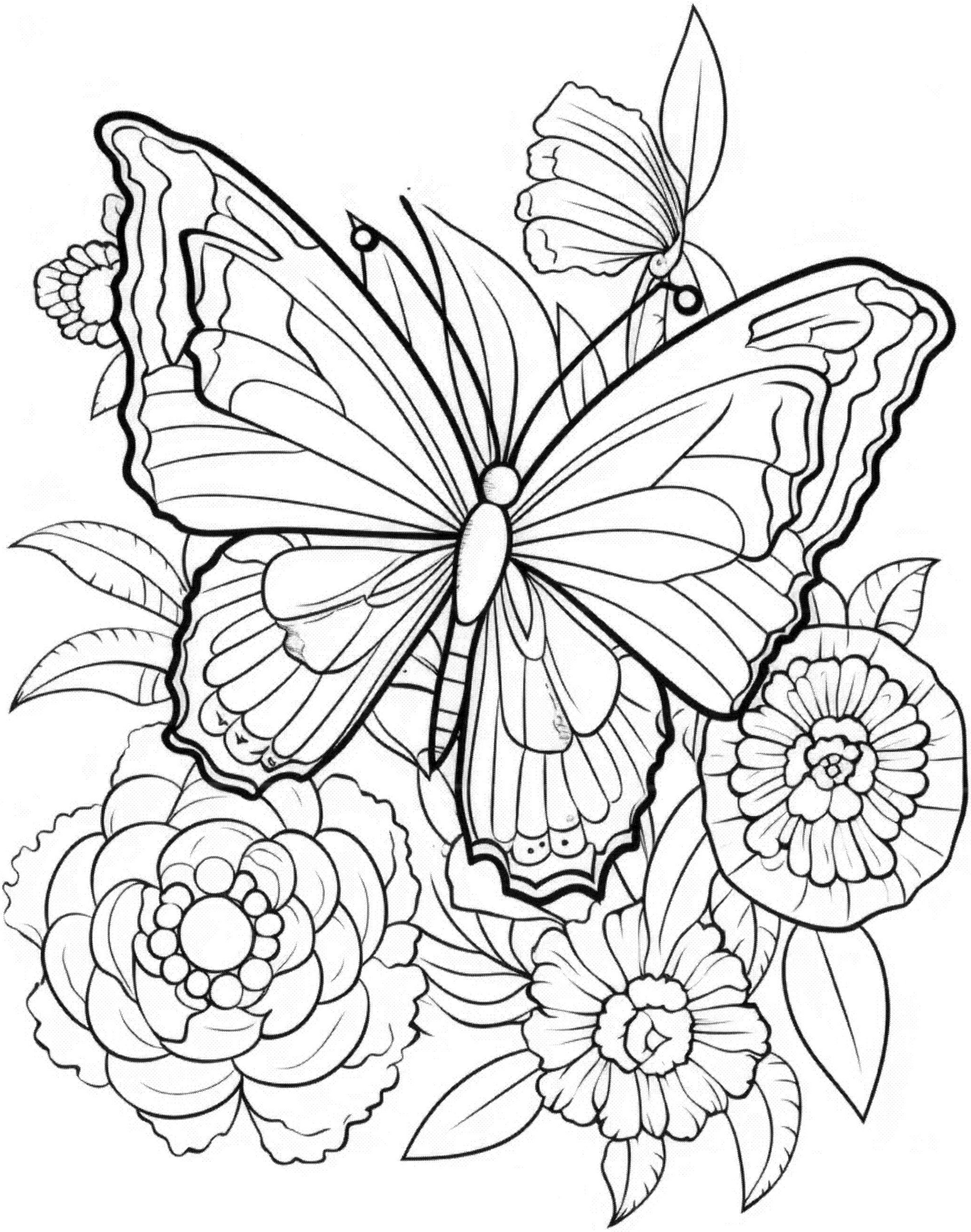

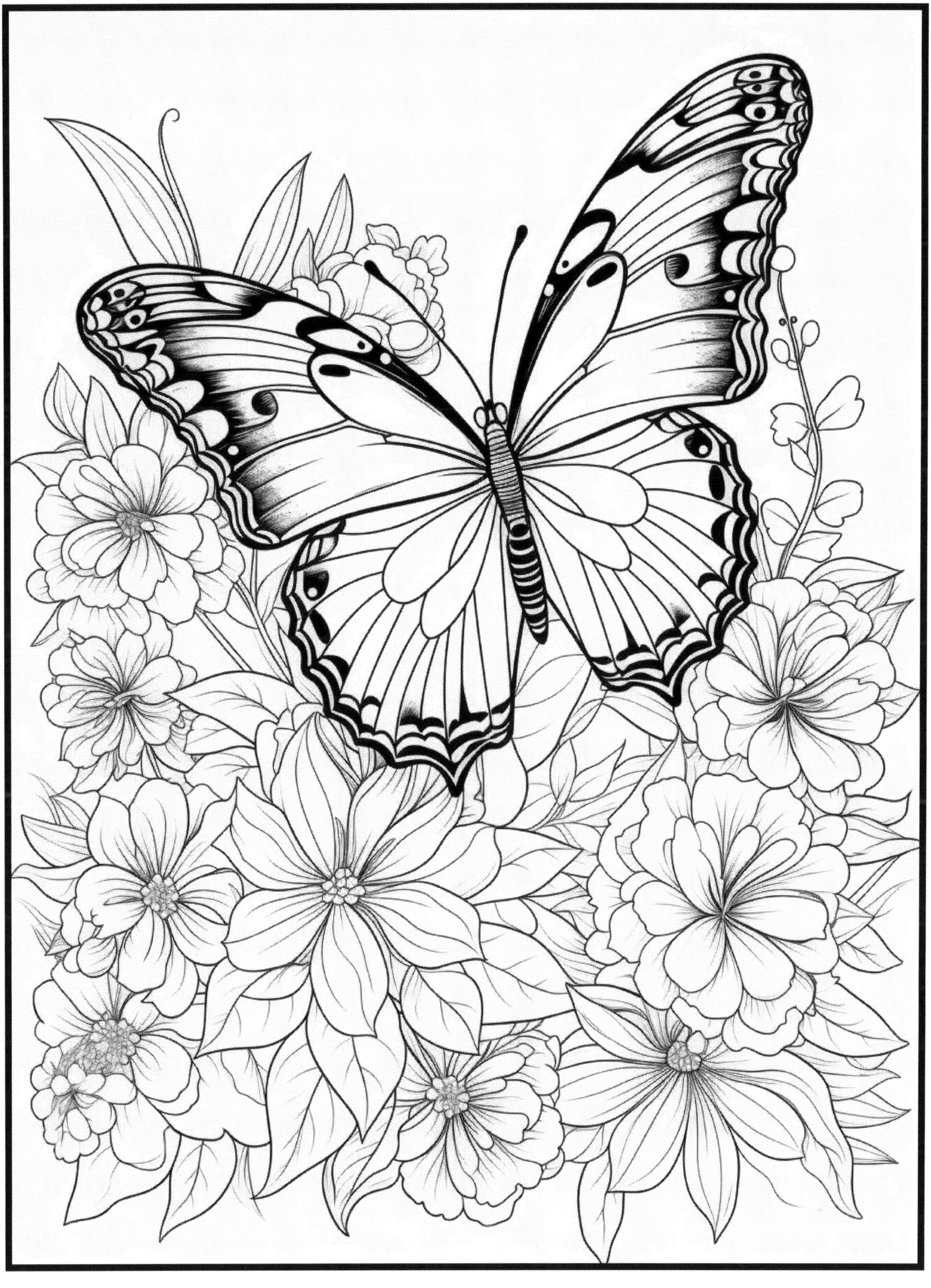

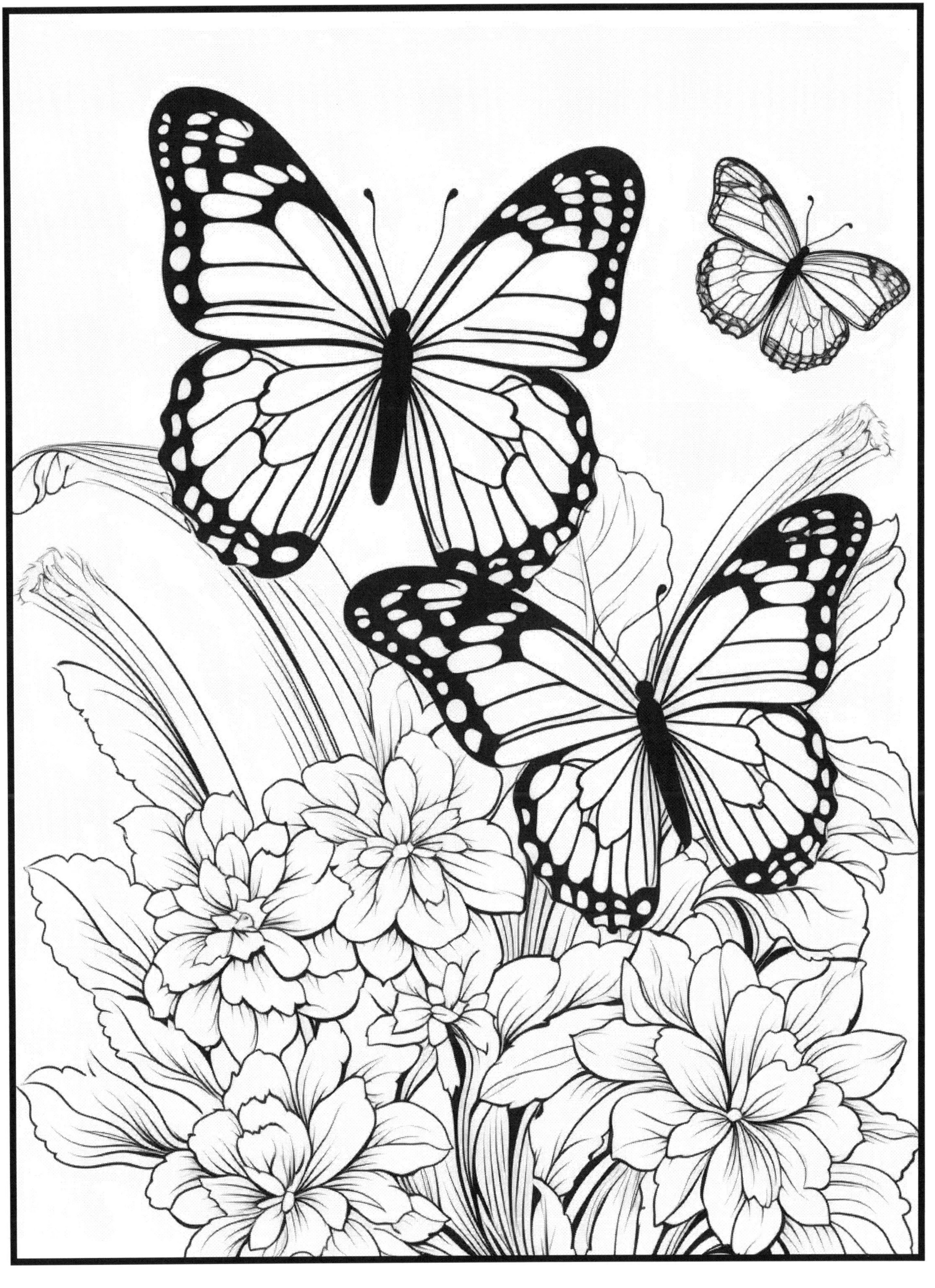

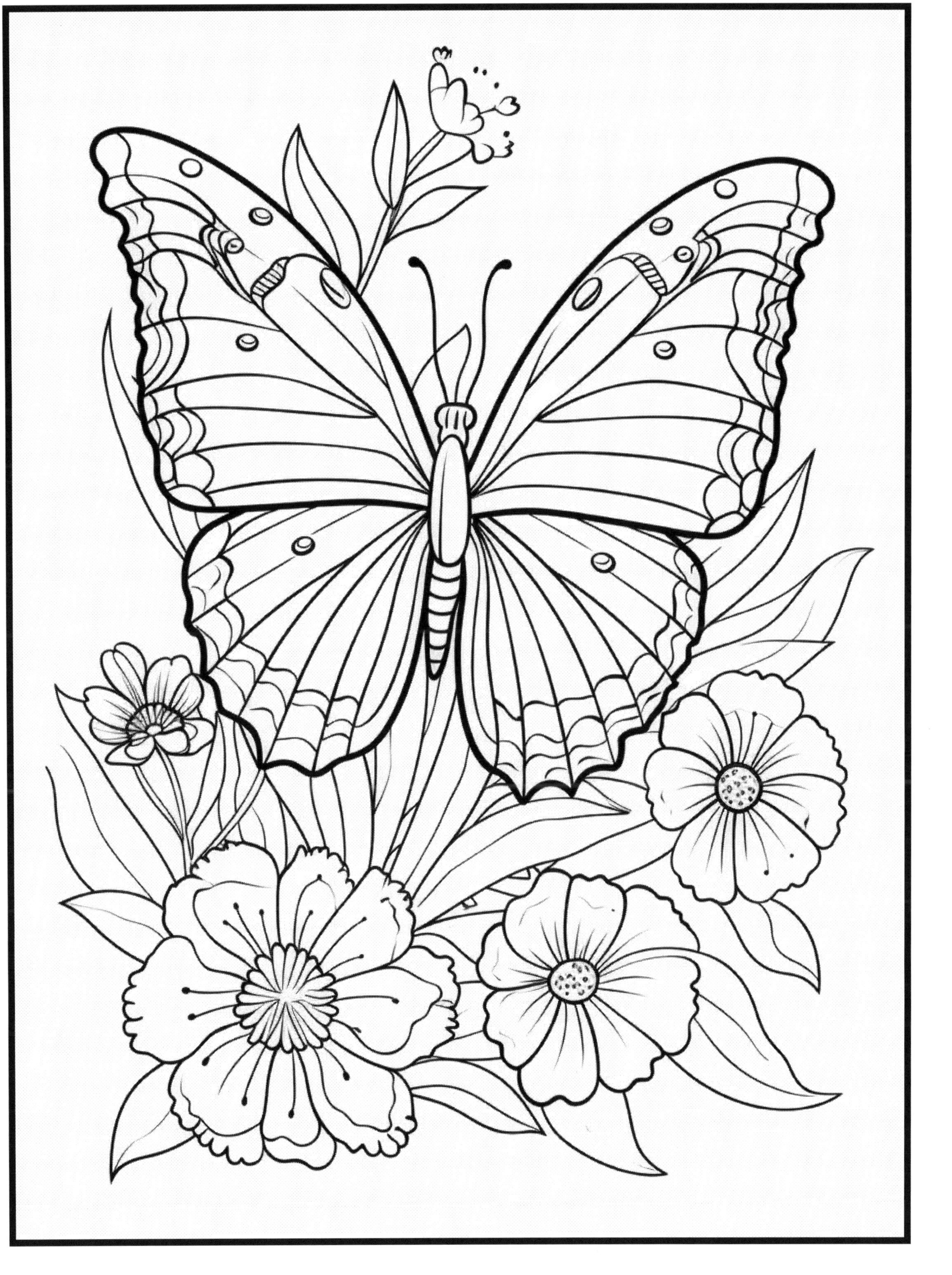

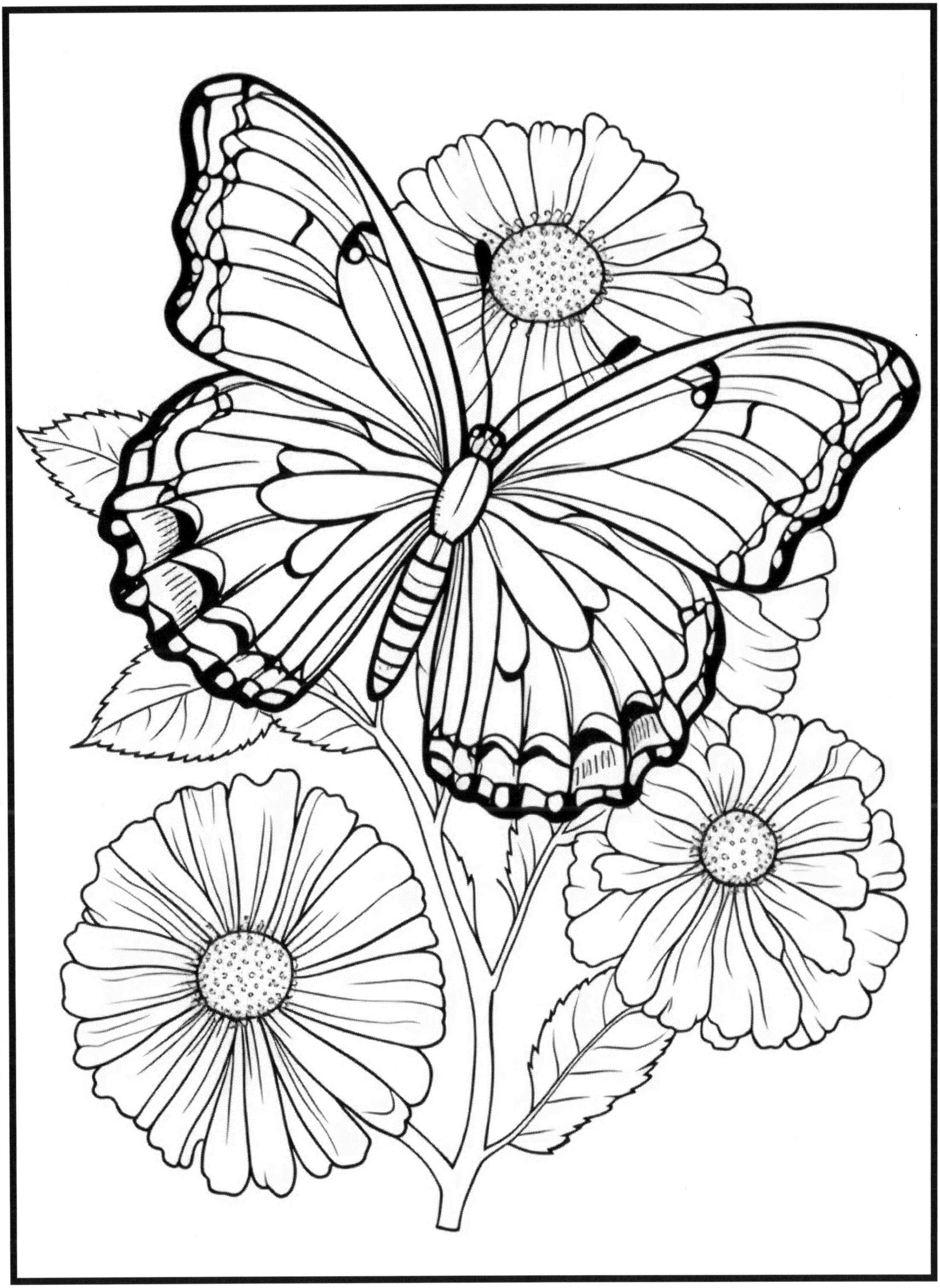

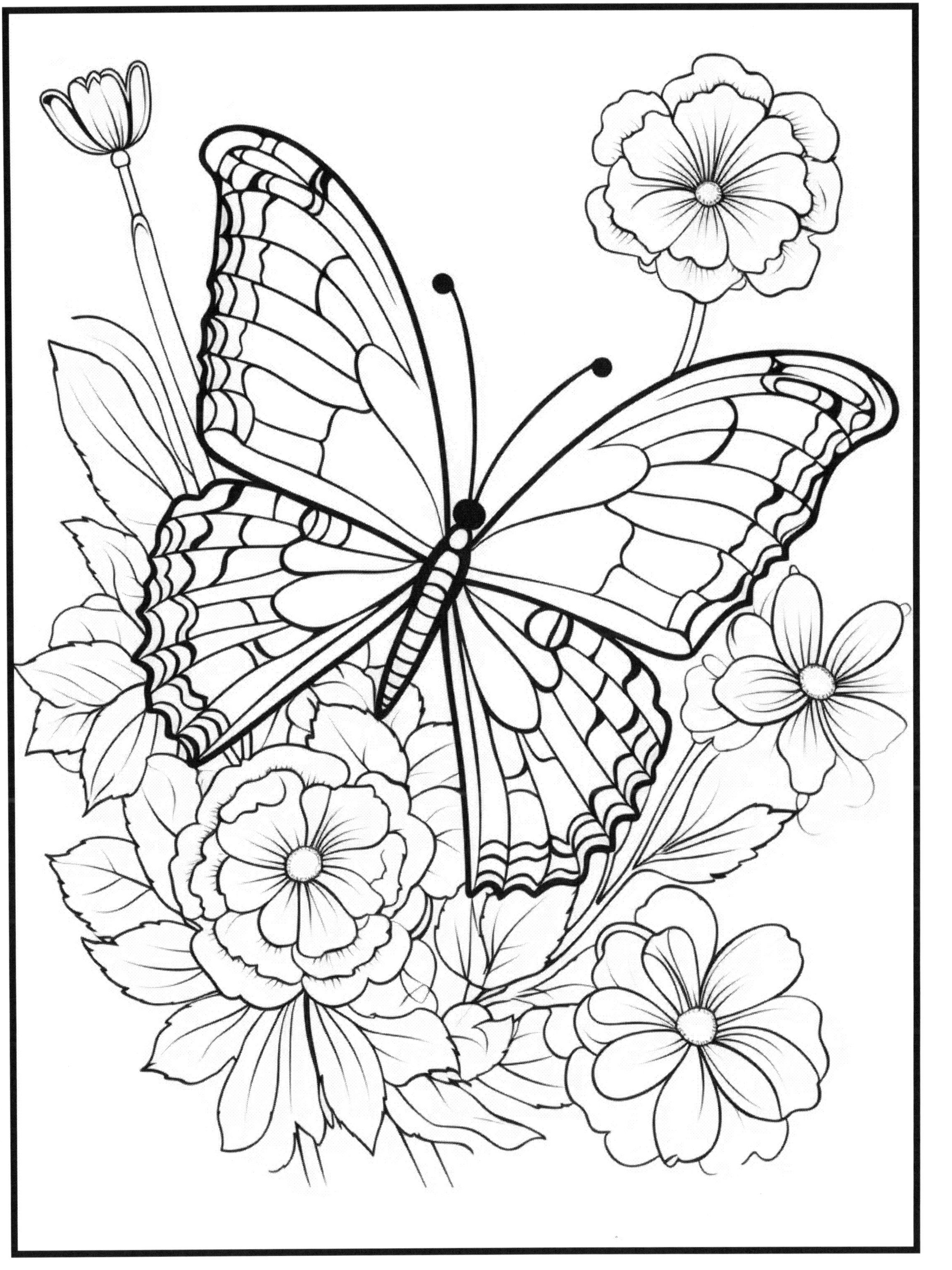

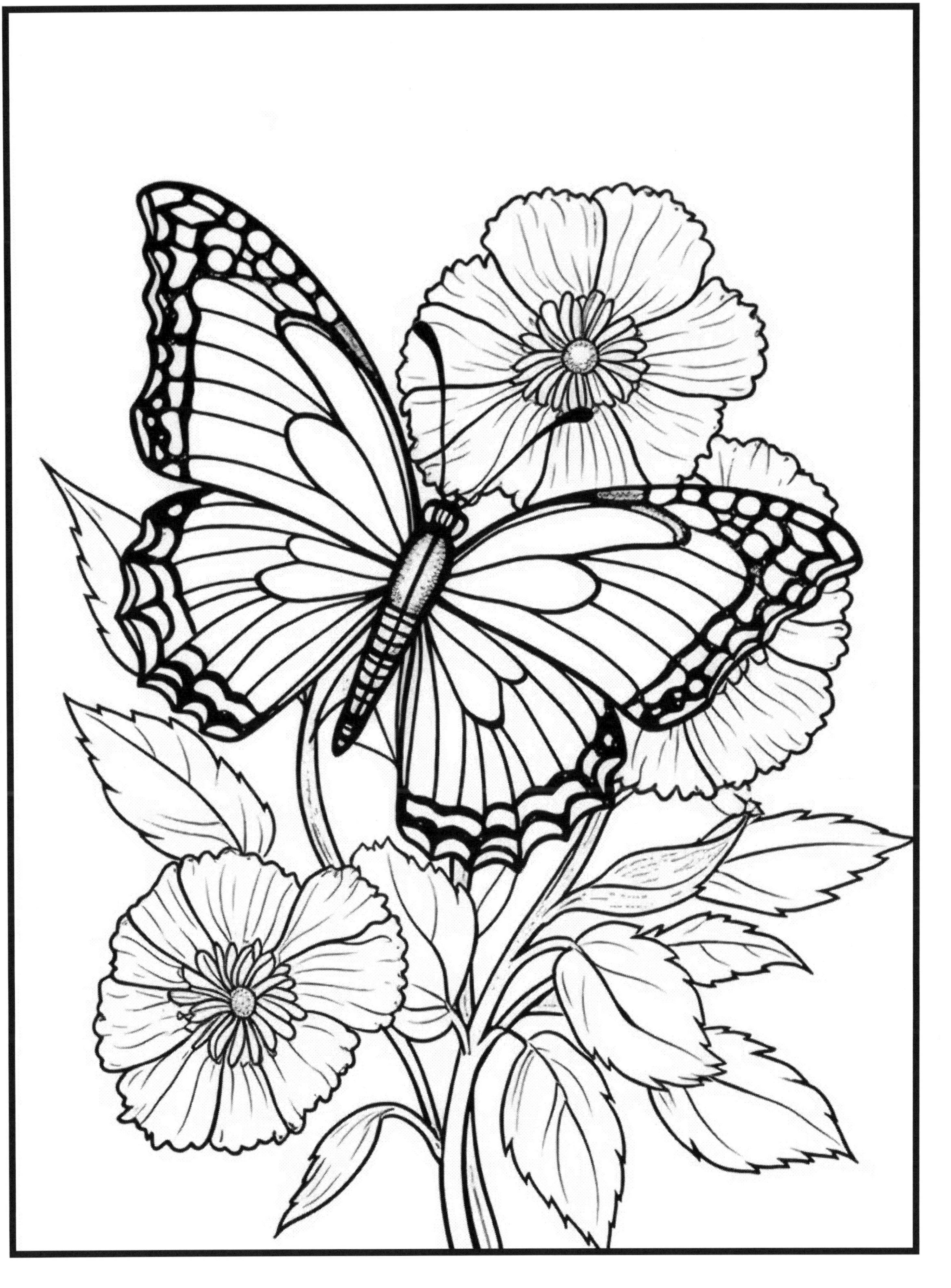

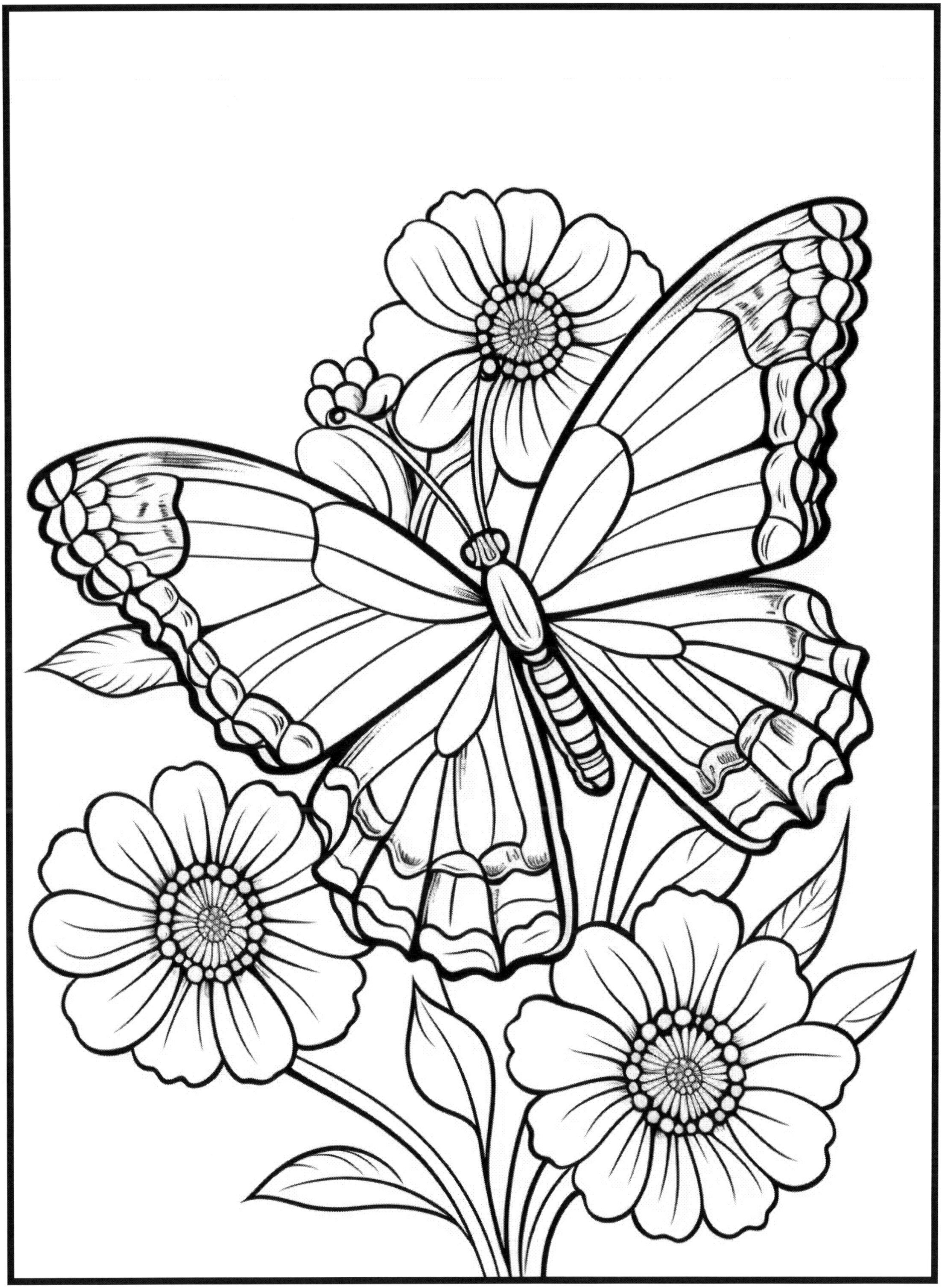

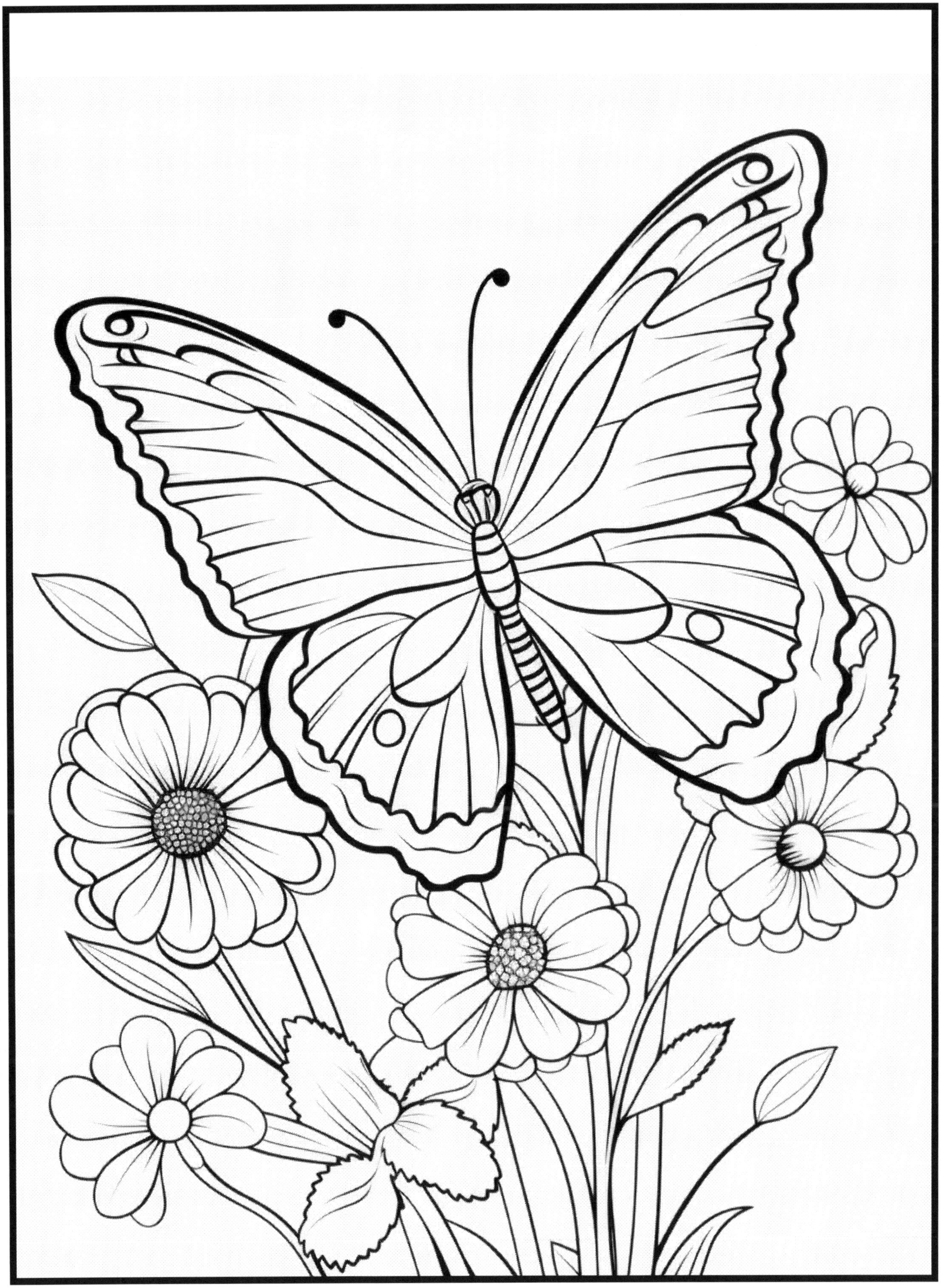

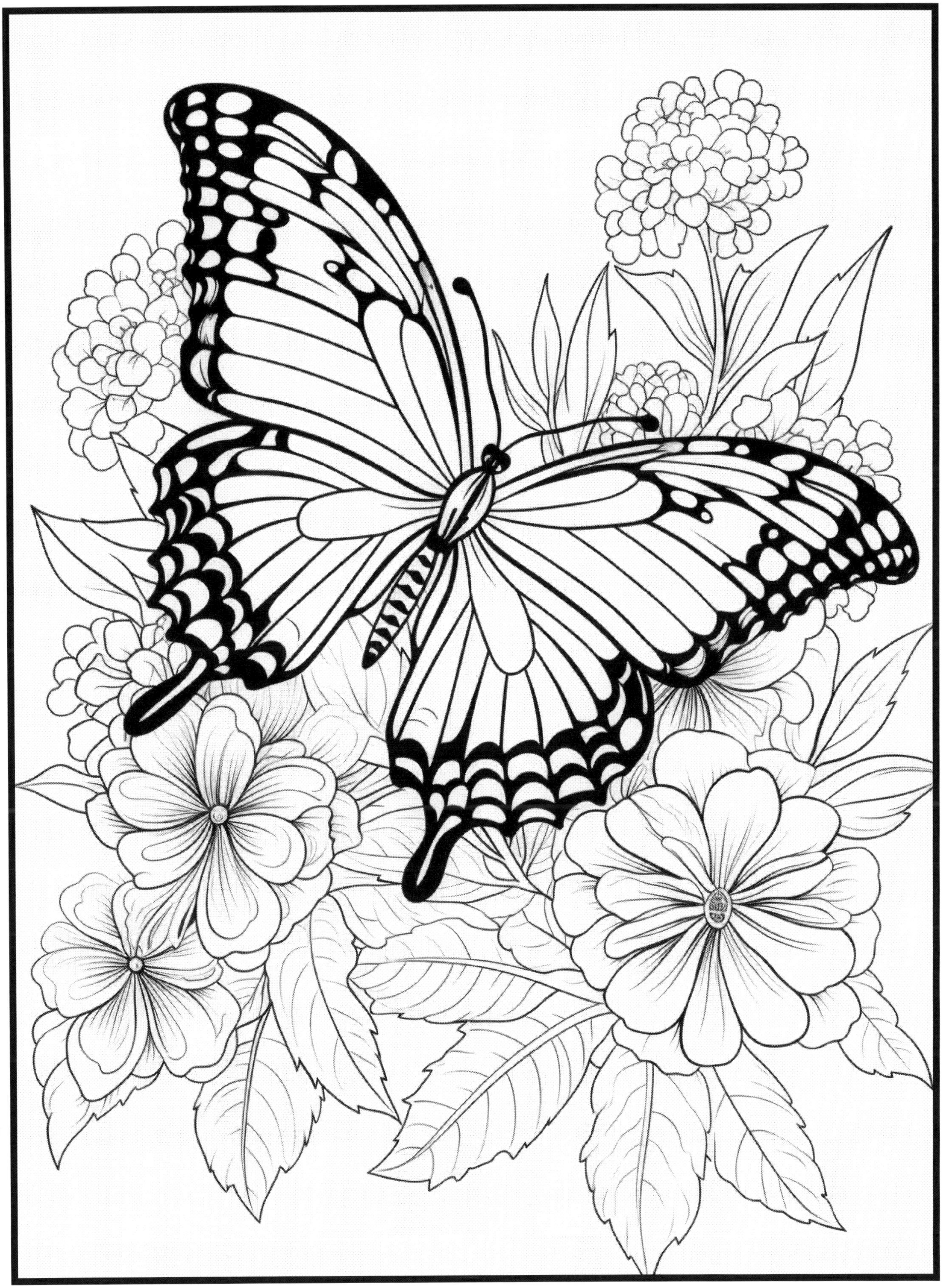

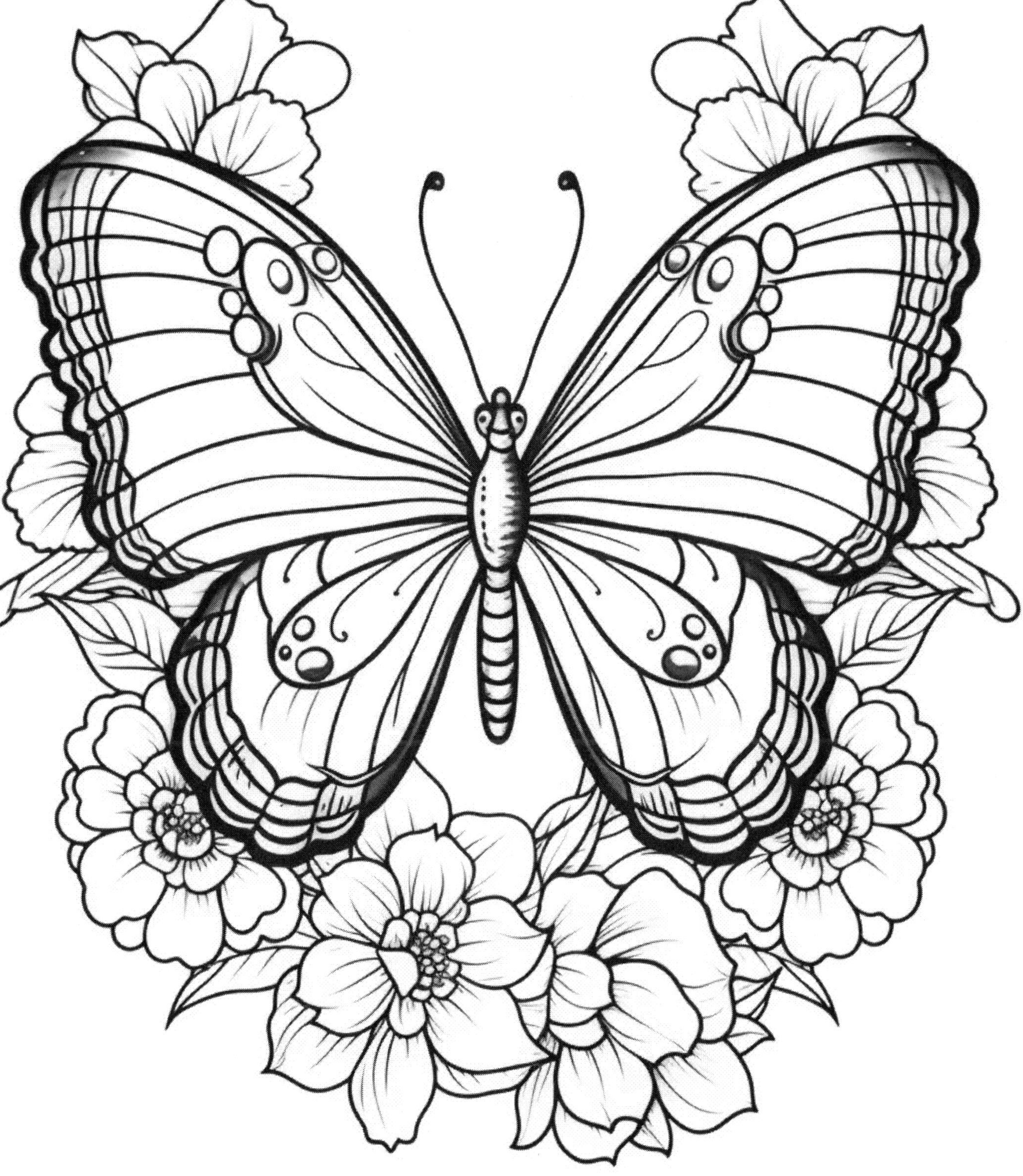

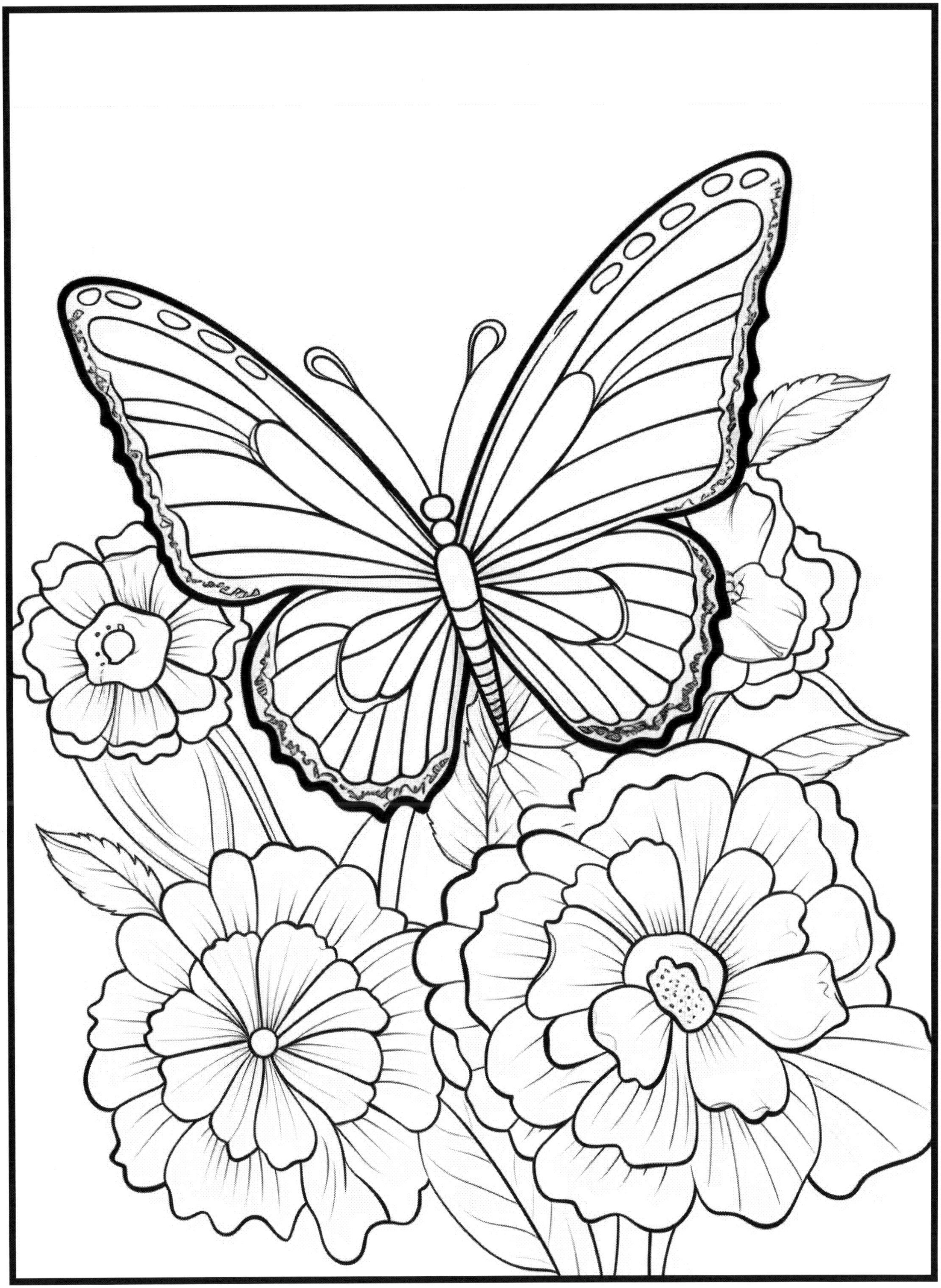

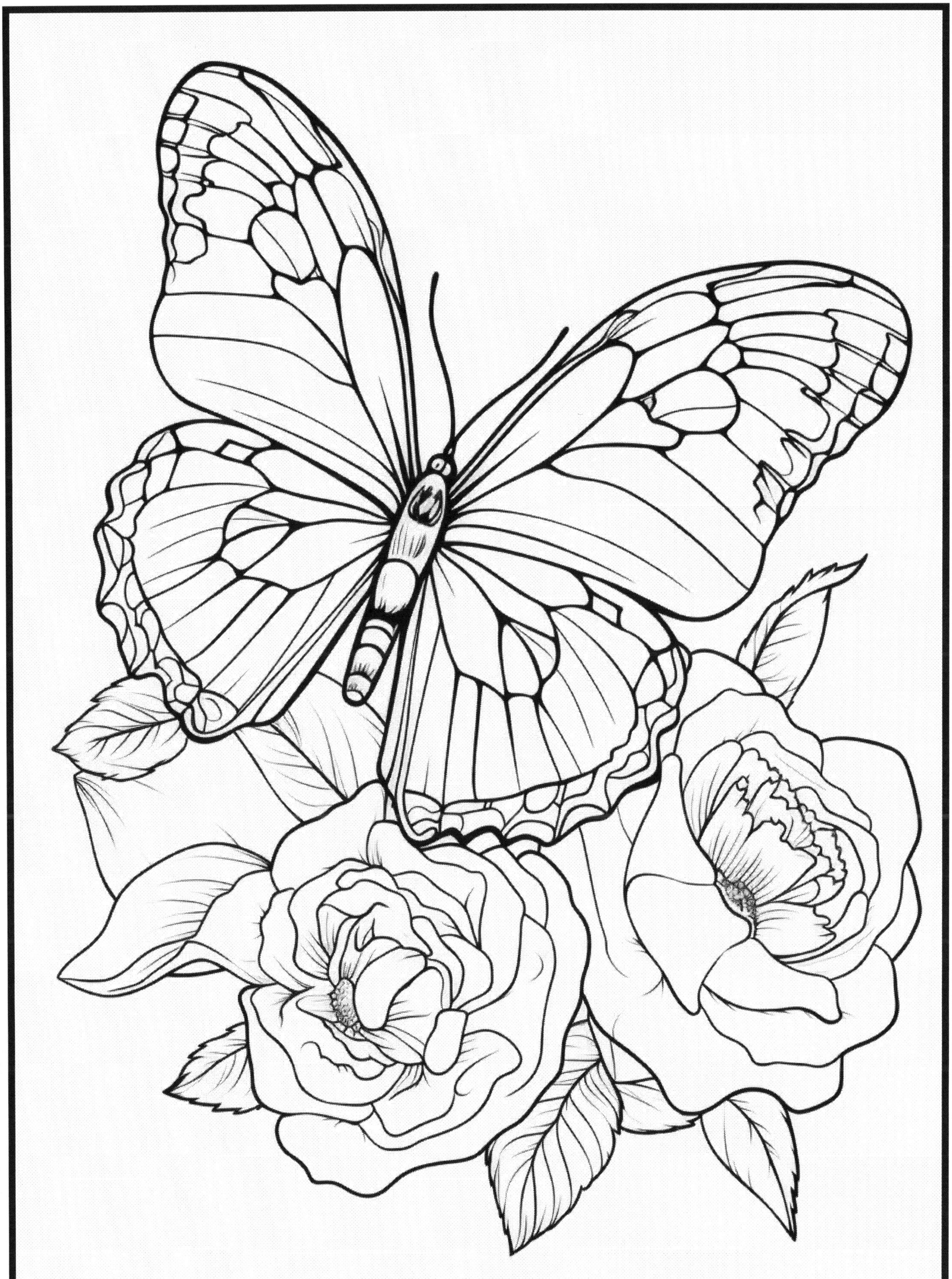

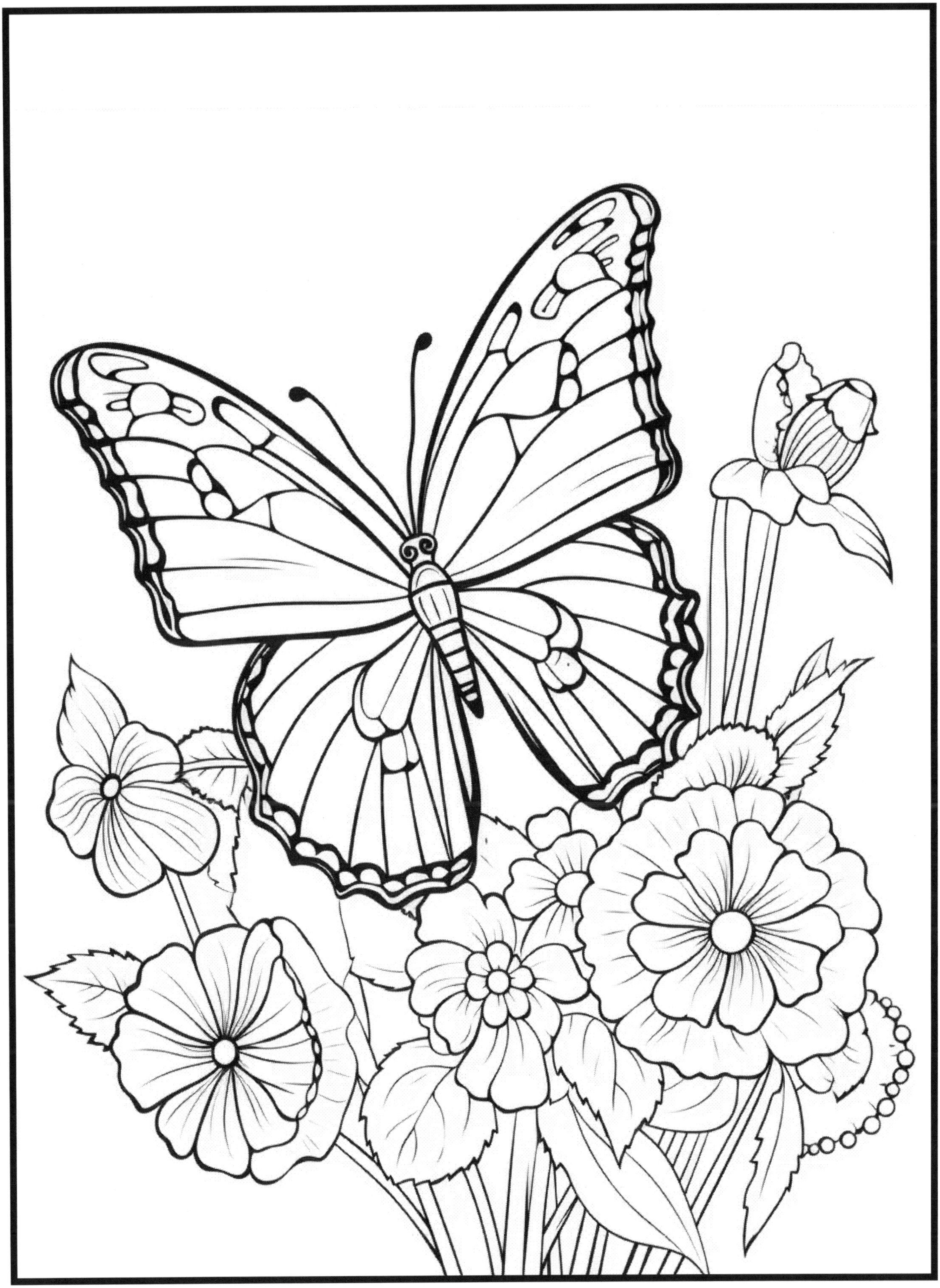

Made in United States
Orlando, FL
22 December 2024

56440307R00057